Thank God I'm Not a Pharisee...or am I?

"Drawing on his rich experience in both church leadership and the market place, John Elzinga exposes those traits and attitudes that keep us from serving God effectively in our relationships and callings--and he offers us wise guidance in pointing us to the path of "grace-full" living."

— **Richard J. Mouw**, PhD
President and Professor of Christian Philosophy
Fuller Theological Seminary

"This is a great book for all who want to avoid the trap of using God's power and truth to manipulate and control others from a self-constructed pedestal made of sorry doctrine."

– **Stephen Arterburn**,
Founder of New Life Ministries

"*Thank God I'm Not a Pharisee...or am I?* ....gives the church a prescription to ward off the sin of self-righteousness."

— **Don Stewart**, Author,
A Case for Christianity
www.simpletruthonline.com

"John has written a book that is clear and helpful about a clear and present danger to the spiritual health of the church. I recommend it."

— **Ken Blue**, Author of *Healing Spiritual Abuse*
www.kenblue.com

"When I see fellow Christians create and develop tools and resources that assist me in this ministry, I not only celebrate them, but also want to pass it on. John Elzinga challenges us as Christians to "hold in check" issues of self-righteousness, legalism, and traditionalism. I want to personally encourage you to take this opportunity to get his most recent study which he entitles: *"Thank God I'm Not a Pharisee…or am I?!"*

—**Dr. Stephen Struikmans**, Founding Pastor
Rancho Community Church

Thank God I'm Not A Pharisee...Or Am I?

*Charting A Path Toward
Grace-Full Living*

John Elzinga

xulon
PRESS

To my wife Claudia...

Who has personally witnessed the Pharisee in me

and has loved me anyway. As an example to all, her

love wades through the muck and mire of real life, sees

past the dirt and grime of my own frailties, and

somehow finds me worth loving.

Contents

Acknowledgements..i

1. What is a Pharisee? 1

2. Pharisees All Around Us!...11

3. The Pharisee In Me 21

4. The Pharisaical Lure 31

5. Seven Types of Pharisees 44

6. Standards and Assumptions...
   the "Not Enough Syndrome" 57

7. Warning Signs and Dangers of the Pharisaical Lure 72

8. Dismantling Pharisaical Mind-Sets 96

9. Blind Guides 118

10. Grace-Full Living 140

Bibliography 155

Notes 159

Acknowledgements

I first and foremost would like to thank my Master and Savior Jesus Christ for providing more grace and mercy to me than I deserve. Frankly, most of the time I don't know what I'm doing…I just follow His lead. And most of the time, it's more like He pushes me into things rather than some kind of clear and easy sign post which says "Turn here."

In the process there are people God has put into my life as a welcome surprise, providing the God-given impetus to challenge me to produce this work. To that end I must thank Lorin Ganske who as owner/manager of NuVision Productions (and also my agent) convinced me that there is a need for this within the evangelical community. His team of talented people includes Daniel Wonacott, who came up with the design and script for Joe Pharisee (in the video series and on this cover); Jon Hudson, who uses his creative skill to edit and make my videos come alive; Justin Leonard, who took a very complex piece of video and spliced it into a friendly 3 minute trailer so everyone can get a taste and feel for what this Pharisee project is all about; and Devan Grell, who faithfully facilitated the arrangement and ordering of all components of the project. Without these people this message would never have been communicated in a palatable way. You guys inspire me!

I want to thank again, Lorin Ganske, along with Tim Josse and our marketing team, who believe in this project so strongly that they communicate to churches, pastors, and booksellers how essential it is that we as evangelical Christians struggle with these issues. They have a heart to get this (and the video series) into as many churches as possible, and for that I am truly grateful.

I would also like to thank Tommy Jolly who edited this book.

I most certainly want to thank my pastor, Dr. Stephen Struikmans, who has faithfully met with me every other week for several years. His encouragement and support spur me on. I appreciate his openness and thoughts concerning this topic, not backing away just because it is a challenging subject.

In addition, Paul Knowles has been a constant source of encouragement to me. He has helped me think through things, even when my emotions cloud out a clear vision.

I would also like to give a special acknowledgement in advance to those churches which have had the courage to invest themselves in the Pharisee Prevention Program facilitated by the use of not only this book but the video/study series by the same name. They have demolished the typical denial/avoidance excuses of DNA (does not apply), and TMOOP (too much on our plate); and have had the foresight to see that the debunking of legalism, self-righteousness, and judgementalism was in fact a *primary* activity of Jesus, and thus should be one of ours as well. I will list your church and keep a running post of your activities, results, and stories on my web site: www.realitycheckresources.com.

I must also thank Dr. Mouw of Fuller Seminary, Stephen Arterburn of New Life Ministries, Don Stewart of The Simple Truth, and Ken Blue author of Healing Spiritual Abuse, and also my pastor, Steve Struikmans for providing their much respected names to endorse this work.

Finally, of all the things I've done in my life; I have never so strongly felt my wife's complete and unwavering support as I have had during this time. Even with all of my doubt and anxiety she has faithfully reminded me that things are done "in God's timing, and in His way." Thank you for your encouragement, sweetheart!

Chapter 1

What is a Pharisee?

"To some who were confident of their own righteousness and looked down on everybody else..." Luke 18:9

Pharisee...the word alone causes us to shiver. The last thing we want to be known as is a Pharisee! We know that Jesus spent a great deal of time speaking against and rebuking the Pharisees. The Pharisees were the great opponents of Jesus and Christianity. Certainly not the type of people we are, or who we associate with... right?

Instinctively, we know that there are modern day Pharisees, we just don't want them to be anywhere near the territory we occupy. We know they're 'out there', but we don't want to recognize that they're here...in our own church fellowship. "Call me anything, just don't call me a Pharisee," is the feeling shared by all evangelical Christians. And so the word conjures up all sorts of images. Images we need to look at and deal with if we are going to be honest and real about our faith and the way we live it out.

The words I hear most often associated with the word Pharisee are; "hypocrites", "legalistic", "judgmental", and "self-righteous." The image is often of some old stodgy guy who has no relation to today, but someone of Jesus' time, someone we don't have to deal with.

We know they're 'out there', but we don't want to recognize that they're here...in our own church fellowship.

We often disassociate ourselves with the Pharisees because of incorrect images and misconceptions of who they were. We feel free, or at least removed from the stereotype we have of the Pharisees and therefore are not really affected by the strong language used by Jesus and others against the Pharisees. We are pretty sure that we are not a Pharisee because of who we think they were. So we must first examine these misconceptions and put some flesh and bones on our definitions of who they were.

Misconceptions

There are many misconceptions about whom the Pharisees were and whom they were not. These misconceptions prevent us from understanding the connections between the Pharisees in Jesus' day, and their relevance to today. The longer we hold on to these misconceptions the more we can ignore their presence in today's world. I find that there are three primary misconceptions and one basic reality regarding who they were.

First, they were not primarily theologians. Although they did concern themselves with what we would call "right doctrine" this was not their primary focus. There were some debates with the Sadducees regarding the issue of the resurrection (whether there was one or not); however, debating theology was not their primary issue.

While the Pharisees and the Sadducees were opponents of each other, for the purposes of this discussion, we will treat them the same. The Sadducees were more politically adept, better educated, and wealthier than the Pharisees. They found a way to adapt to the Greek and

Roman influences of the world and used their political acumen to become influential Jews within the culture of Palestine. Never-the-less, they regarded the influence of Jesus as a threat, even if it was for different reasons.

Secondly, the Pharisees were not insincere or overeducated intellectuals. Their goal was not necessarily intellectual assent; rather, they were more concerned with practical approaches to everyday life. In fact, if they were anything they were sincere.

One of the most important misconceptions we have in all of life is that sincerity somehow comprises truth. We give people high marks for sincerity, but as Mark Twain said, "The secret of success is sincerity. If you can fake that, you've got it made."

We often don't question people if they are sincere. We assume they're correct. And that is a glitch in our thinking, because we also know that we can be sincere, and sincerely wrong. Ironically, sincerity can become the greatest form of deception.

How many of us have been duped unsuspectingly by people who themselves were lost? We become deceived by those who are deceived themselves. We follow those who are lost. We get excited by the passionate promotion of charismatic leaders, even though they may be promoting something that is far from the real truth, or as Francis Schaeffer called it, "True truth." That is to say, often when we hear something that sounds true, perhaps it's packaged in with portions of truth but not the whole truth. Some concept can be 50% true and 50% false, but we will buy the whole package because of the portion that is true.

We don't have to look very far to find examples of this. One of the most famous misquotes of the Bible I have ever heard is, "The Bible says that God helps those who help themselves." This statement sounds pretty good, and if it's presented by someone who is both sincere and "authoritative" we would have a tendency to accept it. But this statement has at least two errors. First, nowhere in the Bible does it say this; and secondly, the truth of the concept is about 50% right. God certainly does want us to live our lives with a sense of stewardship, direction, responsibility and action. However, sometimes God helps those who don't help themselves. God directs in a way that accomplishes His purposes, which sometimes bypass our desired purpose. We need to notice that the Bible says, "The king's heart is in the hand of the Lord; he directs it like a watercourse (river, etc) wherever he pleases" (Prov. 21:1). So the real truth is that while we are to move out in life and take action, God will be the ultimate director in our lives.

But you see the Pharisees goal and job was not intellectual assent. That was the job of the Scribes and the Rabbis. Regarding this, we need to understand how the Pharisees became Pharisees in the first place. They emerged during what we call the "quiet years", the time of approximately 450 BC until the time of John the Baptist. Most commentators say approximately 175 BC. After the Jews were allowed to return from the Babylonian captivity (537 BC) the scribes dedicated themselves to writing down and interpreting the oral tradition.

During this process, they created a complex and vast volume of "laws" and sub-laws, which took the basics of a particular "law" or command, and identified applications of the law to daily life. It was this complexity of life, as defined and interpreted by the Scribes that the Pharisees were committed to "living out in real life". The Pharisees realized that someone needed to dedicate themselves to actually living out these laws, so that they could be an example, and lead the people to become holy and obedient. At least it seems that was their original intent.

Merriam-Webster's definition of a Pharisee is: "a member of a Jewish sect of the intertestamental period noted for strict observance of rites and ceremonies of the written law and for insistence of the validity of their own oral traditions concerning the law." This definition, while highly accurate sounds more like history, something from the bygone years, and not something or someone we have to deal with today.

But this brings us to our third misconception. They were not intentionally deceptive. At least not initially. Their

4

concern originally was to honor God with their obedience and dedication. When Jesus came they did try to trap him deceptively, but that's not how it all got started. We will understand how this works when we get to Chapter Four and discover what I call the "Pharisaical Lure". But for now, understand that deception comes from our inability to be who we want to be. And so at some point we come to the end of ourselves and realize as Paul did, "For what I want to do I do not do, but what I hate I do. And If I do what I do not want to do, I agree that the law is good. As it is, it is no longer I myself who do it, but it is sin living in me" (Rom. 7:15-17). And we along with Paul experience the "hypocrisy of it all."   We discover that we fail, and that mixed in with our spirituality is also our sinfulness. What we set out to do, we are, at first, sincere. But in spite of our sincerity comes the ultimate of deception—we become self-deceived, which was the problem with the Pharisees. Lewis Smedes comments, "Nobody ever says, 'I think I will lie to myself today.' This is the double treachery of self-deception: First we deceive ourselves, and then we convince ourselves that we are not deceiving ourselves."[1]

Who They Were and Who They Are

This brings us to the basic reality of who the Pharisees were. They were self-deceived, spiritual technicians who looked for practical approaches on living the godly life. They were above all things practical, precise, and exact. They wanted to know exactly how to be godly. They detested generalities and broad concepts.

> They were self-deceived, spiritual technicians who looked for practical approaches on living the godly life.

Does this sound like anyone you know? If you ask me, it sounds like the entire evangelical world of which I am a part! To this I plead guilty as charged! Don't we all seek to find practical approaches on living the godly life? Don't we all want to honor God and be obedient? Guilty again!

For the purposes of finding a definition that is real for today's world and for our understanding, let me introduce you with my own definition of what and who a Pharisee is. I call it a working definition because it leads us to the present day realities and applies it to our own lives. For purposes of reminder and reinforcement I have created a *"Pharisee in Me"* card[*] which contains this definition among other statements:

I am a Pharisee when I set up precise standards or actions which I have determined equate to righteousness, holiness, and obedience; and judge others in relationship to my own ability to meet those standards [even when I use Scripture].

Quite frankly, there is a lot I don't like about this definition, but try as I would I can't bring myself to modify it. This definition rattles my cage and chaps my hide. It makes me feel uneasy, uncomfortable, and restless.

Primarily this is because I am admitting that I am a Pharisee. To make this definition 'work' I have to own it. So when I read "I am a Pharisee" I am admitting that these things are true of me. It is constructive to look at and admit that I---through my own sense of conviction and experiences—set up my own system of righteousness, my own rules and guidelines. Then I judge others in comparison to my own ability to meet those standards. But the real rub is that this can include "even when I use Scripture!" It's one thing to claim that I set up my own standards, it's a whole other thing to claim that I do this even when I use Scripture.

How do I know this to be true? How can I make a claim like this? Well, simply put, if this is what the Pharisees and the Sadducees did, then what makes you think that we don't do this as well?

You can read about such a situation in Matthew 19:3-9. Here we find the Pharisees trying to "test" Jesus

---

[*] You can order a Pharisee In Me card from *Reality Check Resources*, www.realitycheckresources.com

regarding to what he believed regarding divorce and then trying to "trap" him regarding what Moses said about the subject. This was part of their M.O. in how they used Scripture. And, it is something we are pretty good at in the evangelical world.

In an argument, or "discussion" have you ever used a text of Scripture to prove your point? Proof texting is our M.O. In an attempt to do what is right we end up proof texting our way through life so we can justify what we think is right. Armed with proof texts I've seen Christians justify anything from divorce, to rock throwing, to 'shunning', to what clothes we wear. What makes this so bad is that Scripture may indeed say something close to "your point", but the intent of "your" Scriptural reference is not the point of the Scripture referenced! In other words, we take Scriptures out of context so that it can prove our point. Out of context we can make the Scriptures say almost anything. Martin Luther said, "With Scripture I can prove that bad beer is better than good wine."

Regarding the concept of divorce, the Pharisees were referencing Deuteronomy 24:1-4. They misused the "allowance" for divorce to the point that a man could divorce his wife for virtually anything. If he didn't like the way she cooked meals, he could divorce her. If he grew tired of her, he could divorce her. After all, it was "allowed" in Scripture! Jesus was pointing out that they got it wrong. It wasn't that it was allowed because it was okay; rather, it was permitted because of the "hardness of hearts" and even then, Jesus reminded them that it was only "acceptable" in the case of marital infidelity. They twisted it around to say something quite different, something that served *their* purposes. Over the years, Christians have used Scripture to prove that the world is flat, that slavery is okay, or that God's goal is for you to live in prosperity.

Scripture twisting is pretty easy to understand if we simply look at a Scripture that has no impact upon us today, and no self-righteous pressure. Revelation 7:1 says, "After this I saw four angels standing at the four corners of the earth…"(NIV). The thinking was that if angels were standing on four corners then certainly that meant that the world was flat. You can only have corners on a flat or cubic surface. It says "corners" in the Bible; therefore, the world is flat. The Bible says it! Well, that misunderstanding of Scripture prevented the discovery of the "new world" for hundreds of years. Even thinking of launching out was considered blasphemous!

While the above example is inconsequential to us, there are many other instances in which Scripture twisting has created pharisaical and condescending attitudes towards others. The monastic movement, in its attempt to not be "of" the world, found a way to remove itself from the world which then of course violated the offsetting command to be "in" the world. Scripture twisting often emphasizes one Scripture at the cost of another; thus not considering the whole Word but only a part of the Word which usually conforms to our view point. What would happen for example, if we took Acts 2:46, "*Every day* they continued to meet together;" 2 Corinthians 6:14, "Do not be yoked together with unbelievers...what *fellowship* can light have with darkness;" and 1 John 2:15, "Do not love the world or anything in the world;" and combined them to form a position on how we are to relate with the world and live out our lives within the body of Christ? Here's what you would get: believers are to meet together every day, we should not fellowship with unbelievers, and that we should not love the world. The result being that most believers wouldn't be able to work (certainly not the millions of commuters) productively in their jobs because they always need to get home in time to get to the "meeting;" Christians wouldn't be able to have a relationship with unbelievers, and we would despise the world, thus losing our leverage upon it. And if you think this is an exaggeration and not real, think again. I knew of someone who belonged to a group of believers who felt exactly this way; in fact he felt that he couldn't even have

> Pharisees are especially talented at twisting Scripture; it's their favorite past time!

lunch with me, not knowing if I was a "real" believer or not (even though I told him I was a Christian, he felt he could only be sure of those within his own fellowship)! You see, Pharisees are especially talented at twisting Scripture; it's their favorite past time! It is their strategic initiative to control the rules of the game.

Pharisees are standard bearers, line drawers, righteousness seekers, holiness displayers, obedience demanders, judging evaluators, accountability cops, Scripture twisters, spiritual intimidators, and authority grabbers. They promote the letter of the law over the spirit of the law, design a life no one can live except themselves, model their spirituality for all to see, love to be heard, are the first to stand up and pray, and engage in a constant game of spiritual one-upmanship. Their sincerity is contrived, they are proud of their humility, they are the biggest "doers" around, they are at church every time the door opens, they study the Bible like no other, they can quote Scripture left and right; and they always, always, believe they are right!

> Pharisees want to make sure you are obedient, that you don't disagree with them…

Pharisees want to make sure you are living how you should, that you don't slip up, they are perpetually "concerned" about you and your faith, they will be happy to call something to your attention if you are not doing it "enough," and if they can't get your attention they'll be glad to let others knowing how you're doing, or not doing, as the case may be.

In addition, Pharisees what to make sure you are obedient, that you don't disagree with them, that real unity is the acceptance of their position and that all other dissenters have "another agenda," that they are God's faithful, directors, leaders, and dispensers of the truth, and so ultimately they create blindly devoted followers. Did I leave anyone out? If so, by the end of this book, you will discover how real Pharisees are in our evangelical world. It's frightening how real they are, and even more frightening as we examine their patterns and trends and how common they are. Yet, it is dangerous to leave this part of our evangelical world unexamined because to not confront these realities we authorize their existence. We perpetuate the very things we detest!

And so we see who the Pharisees really were, and who they really are. As Lewis Smedes comments,

> The Pharisees were good people, but some of them were good only in a shallow, legalistic sort of way. For them life was a serious game. The object was to score points with God. Score enough points and you win. Score too few and you lose. So the Pharisees divided all the people they knew into two groups: winners and losers in the game of getting on with God. [2]

This comment is too close for comfort leading us into the next question: "where do we find these modern day Pharisees?" And we all sigh, "Not around here I hope...?"

Chapter 2

Pharisees All Around Us!

The Pharisees gathered-Matthew 22:41;
the Pharisees went out -Matthew 22:15

One of the goals of this book is to understand and recognize the frightening reality that the Pharisees weren't just the spiritual thugs of Jesus' day, but that they are alive and well today. Pharisees are all around us. Everywhere we go within our evangelical community we will find them.

This is a hard pill to swallow, but the fact is that we don't have to look far...all we have to do is look in the mirror. Everywhere we find the pursuit of righteousness, holiness, and obedience, we will find modern day Pharisees. Now is as good a time as any to face this reality. The best way to do this is to identify what a Pharisaical Attitude might look like. And before we find these attitudes in ourselves it is easier to identify when we have encountered others in the act of being Pharisaical. That's right. For the purposes of identifying Pharisaical Attitudes you have permission to think about, talk about, and write down instances and occasions when you have seen the Pharisaical Attitude in others. This should be fairly easy to do because I believe we all have encountered many Pharisees in our lives.

Pharisaical encounters

In our video series we created a character we affectionately called Joe Pharisee. In the beginning we see Joe, as a leader of a congregation, talking about how it is more spiritual to wear holy sandals (like he does) than wearing tennis shoes. It seems that tennis shoes "offended" him since he felt it was unspiritual to wear such things to church. Joe was "exhorting" them to wear sandals and not wear tennis shoes.

In my DVD series I relate this to what I experienced growing up in the church. When I grew up you had to wear a suit and tie when you went to church because the concept was that this was giving God your best. If you went to church you wanted to honor God with your best, and your best meant a suit and tie. To wear anything other than a suit and tie was not your best and therefore not honoring to God. If someone showed up in Dockers (or the equivalent) or worse yet, jeans, they would not be seen as honoring God with their best, and were therefore frowned upon.

> Pharisees are all around us. Everywhere we go within our evangelical community we will find them.

The issue of what clothes you wear has definitely been a source of conflict, tension, and Pharisaical attitudes within the evangelical church. It still is today in many "traditional" churches. Today, you have shorts and sandals churches, suit and tie churches, casual wear churches, emergent churches where you might find guys with tattoos and ear rings; but rarely do you find a blend within these churches. How many churches do you know of where you will find the variety of clothing I just discussed all within the same service? Odds are that if someone with a t-shirt, shorts, and sandals showed up in a suit and tie church they probably wouldn't attend again…they wouldn't feel comfortable.

But not feeling comfortable is too light of a statement. The truth is that they would probably feel judged and frowned upon. They would perceive and feel a very real Pharisaical attitude present. You can feel it, like a thousand eyes focusing in on you. You are sure everyone is watching you, and that they don't like what they see.

I grew up in the late 60's when the hippie generation was popular. In tune with this cultural change was the appearance of long hair on guys. Christians were not exempt from wanting to fit in, and soon you found Christian young men showing up in churches with long hair. Although my hair was not particularly long, I distinctly remember an incident when an older gentleman from our church confronted a teenager who had long hair in the narthex of the church and anxiously gave him money "to go and get a hair cut, so you can look decent and respectable". (ironically, the guy who did this was bald!)

Question: what was he conveying to this young man about the love and grace of God (I do not believe this young man was a confessing Christian at the time)? What was the belief of the older gentleman about requirements of spirituality? What was the attitude he conveyed? How did the young man feel? What do you think his perception was regarding God's love and acceptance? And here's the big question: based upon these kinds of actions, do you think this young man eventually became a Christian?

> Did you ever feel like you were being trapped and cornered by others in the reality of your own sin; worse yet, put down just being who you are?

Pharisaical encounters Identified

Finding others slip up is the ultimate Pharisaical high. It pumps self-righteous adrenalin through our bodies. And we start looking for things in others just as the Pharisees did: "Then the Pharisees went out and laid plans to trap him [Jesus] in his words." (Matthew 22:15). Did you ever feel like you were being trapped and cornered by others in the reality of your own sin; worse yet, put down just being who you are?

And so before we go any farther, I would like you to take a minute to identify times or experiences in which you have encountered others being Pharisaical. What was the issue or event? What was the attitude that was conveyed or projected? And, most importantly, how did it make you feel?

Issues   Attitudes   Feelings

Now that you have had a chance to identify a few pharisaical encounters yourself we can talk about common issues that arouse the spirit of self-righteousness, condemnation, disfavor, and spiritual superiority.

The style of ministry for example is a present bone of contention between what I will call traditionalist and those looking for some contemporary forms of worship. Particularly, the issue is how we worship. Hymns seem to be the favorite medium of those preferring a more formal and traditional style of worship, while contemporary praise music being favored by the younger and larger majority of worshipers. Even at that, there are divisions among the contemporary set, because with the emergent generation seeks an even more contemporary style which includes volume, pace, and atmosphere.

This is no small matter since it is the cause of division and tension, even to the point of dividing churches. Traditional hymns have a certain reverence to them, creating a 'feeling' of honor for God the most High, while contemporary praise music ignites passion and connection to God the most nigh.

The problem is that neither group sees it the way the other does. The traditionalists feel that the contemporary music is trite, light, and almost irreverent. "Why sing something that is merely a chorus over and over again…it has no substance"? So goes the comments from that group. The more contemporary group would say that hymns are boring, dull, lethargic, and complicated. "Who talks like that today?" "No one plays the organ any more!" These are typical comments regarding hymns, reflecting upon the old English style of music, with the 'thees' and 'thous' in-tact, which seems to dominate the older hymns. This style is quite foreign to the younger group, but precious to the older group. And so the issue persists.

But these are just difference of opinions. What is the harm of either one? A legitimate question and the right one I might add. However, to the staunch holders of each position it becomes a pharisaical issue. The traditionalist looks down upon the contemporary with a kind of "spite" in that they feel that the contemporary creates irreverence towards God...a trivialization of our creator God who is high and holy. Their spite comes out in many forms: grumbling, looks of disgust, and even worse, accusations of rebellion and even questioning their spirituality. If the traditionalists are in positions of power and influence in a changing congregation they will try to prevent those that desire contemporary worship from gaining any influence and will fight the implementation of the new style at that church. Simply put, it seems that their perspective is that they are more mature, honoring to God, more holy, and more spiritual than the contemporary Christians. They are honoring the God who is most high, while the younger group is not. What does this attitude sound like to you?

The contemporary gang, however, isn't immune from a Pharisaical attitude. They view the traditionalists as lacking passion, or even worse, as not loving the Lord as they do. They may even feel that they are dry and lukewarm Christians, lacking "power or vibrancy in their life. What does this attitude sound like to you?

Another issue that has Pharisaical overtones is the issue of "spiritual gifts," particularly what are known as charismatic gifts of the spirit. Few things have divided the evangelical church more over the years than this issue. This is first and foremost a theological and doctrinal issue. Its root cause is regarding how you understand and interpret the Scriptures. These are ongoing things that the church universal needs to dialogue, debate, and wrestle with. But the problem is that it seldom happens, that is, respectable debate. It crosses the line between doctrinal disagreement to spiritual disgust and disfavor.

Again, those that hold the position that you must have a "second baptism" and be baptized by the Holy Spirit to get your spiritual anointing and your spiritual gift, hold in great disfavor those who believe that when they received Jesus Christ they also received and accepted the whole package, the unity of the Trinity: Father, Son, and Holy Spirit.

Those holding the position of charismatic gifts often look down upon those who don't: "if you don't have a prayer language you are just half a Christian." Although they might not explicitly say this, that is what is communicated. Spiritual arrogance usually comes from a frame of reference that "you must have what I have" (whether or not it's completely Scriptural). Yet the Apostle Paul specifically speaks against this kind of attitude in 1 Corinthians 13:1-2 when he says basically that if love isn't your motivation, don't do it, don't force it, and don't promote it. When you read 1 Corinthians 12, 13, and14 together, within the context of love, you will see that it's not the specific gift that you have that makes you spiritual. In fact, arrogantly holding one gift over the other may negate your gift.[1] Because Paul says, "If I speak in the tongues of men and of angels, but have not love, I am only a resounding gong or a clanging cymbal..." (1 Cor. 13:1) A gong and cymbal clashing symbolizes the concept that you may be speaking so loud no one can hear you! You may be forcing an issue upon someone who has no need of it! Basically, a forced issue is a non-issue. Accept everyone, with who they are and with the gift they have, lovingly. Then go ahead an exercise your gift, whatever it may be.

Possibly one of the most common sources of Pharisaical attitudes comes from "moral" questions of how we live our life. Specifically, "Christians don't drink, don't dance, and don't go to movies." Much of this conflict originates from those who hail from "holiness" traditions. In seeking to be pure and spotless...to keep unstained from the worlds pleasures, and to be a good witness produces standards of behavior that somehow are supposed to define what is acceptable and unacceptable. The problem is that these issues are Biblical grey areas and not explicit. We will discuss this later and in more detail, but briefly consider attitudes, attacks, and accusations that are often projected by those who feel that one behavior in particular is unacceptable and even un-Christian.

For example, if you are a Christian who believes there is nothing wrong with having a drink such as a glass of wine with dinner, yet are in a church fellowship where this is either "frowned upon" or is questionable, have you ever found yourself looking around a restaurant to see who might be there before you ordered a drink? What motivated that apprehension? What was your fear? That you would be "caught"? That you are doing something wrong? That you would be looked down on? Considered sinning? Not spiritual? Or even worse condemned (from their point of view) or even kept from leadership at that church fellowship because you had a drink, which you don't think is wrong?

If you are a Christian or Christian leader who believes that Christians "shouldn't" drink; have you ever caught yourself "catching" someone who is in your church fellowship having a drink at a restaurant and thinking less of them for it? Questioning their spirituality? Thinking they are a loose or immature Christian? Think that they are sinning? Perhaps you even felt more strongly about it, and felt that you must confront this person with their sin!

> What was your fear? That you would be "caught"? That you are doing something wrong? That you would be looked down on? Considered sinning? Not spiritual?

Before you jump ahead to rationalize or justify your position please note we will deal with this question in detail in the section I call "stumbling over the stumbling block" in Chapter Eight. This chapter and section are about discovering the feelings and attitude associated with self-righteousness and judgementalism.

Where were the Pharisees? "The Pharisees gathered" (Matt. 22:41); "the Pharisees went out" (Matt. 22:15). It appears that they got together to complain about the sinners out there, then they went out to find and confront more. They were here, there, and everywhere. And so it is today! We've all encountered them in some form, and regarding some issue. Because of this, we need to think in terms of finding a way to deter any form of self-righteousness and judgementalism. We need to find a way to prevent Pharisees from gaining an upper hand in our spiritual lives and in our fellowships. We need to find a way

19

to make sure, we don't become Pharisees ourselves. We need some form of Pharisee prevention.

Pharisee Prevention

It is for this reason that we have created two "teaching" or reinforcement aids: the *Pharisee Prevention Handbook* and the *"Pharisee In Me"* card. With these props you are challenged to do the following:

1. Take the concepts your have identified on page 15 and transfer them into the *Pharisee Prevention Handbook* under the section "Pharisees All Around." Use this to stimulate your thinking and awareness. During the week, you may be able to identify other issues that have come up that you witness are pharisaical. Fill in this section.

2. Take your *Pharisee In Me* card with you at all times. Use this as your constant reminder or your own tendency to be Pharisaical. Particularly review the definition of what a Pharisee, reading "I am a Pharisee…" This will help your awareness.

3. If (when) you discover the reality of the *Pharisee In Me*, check your card and enter the issue in your *Pharisee Prevention Handbook*.

These tools are to be used as your reminders that not only are there Pharisees all around—it's not just about those hypocrites out there—but that there is a Pharisee in me! Now we need to look in the mirror for a moment. The next chapter will be your mirror.

Chapter 3

The Pharisee In Me!

"The Pharisee stood up and prayed about himself: 'God, I thank you that I am not like other men...'" Luke 18:11

Sooner or later, I believe we all come face to face with our own self-righteousness and legalism. For most of us I believe that this discovery comes by surprise, as we relate to the Christian community of which we are a part. As you read about my own story it should become clear that the surprise is that it can happen in the midst of our own sense of excitement, commitment, and discipline.

My Story

I first faced the reality of my own Pharisaicalism at the end of my freshman year in college. I had left my home in northwest Indiana to go to Calvin College in Grand Rapids, Michigan. This was to be a natural extension of my Christian education since I had gone to Christian grade and high schools. Calvin was and is a fantastic Christian college and I owe to Calvin a lot in terms of my Christian world and life view. However, while there one of my extra-curricular activities was to get involved in the Navigators. The Navigators is a Christian para church ministry which ministers primarily to college students as well as other realms such as the military. They have a strong evangelistic emphasis but really focus its efforts on the discipleship of collage students on campuses all across the nation. As part of their discipleship approach they get students involved in Bible study, fellowship, prayer, evangelism, and Scripture memory. Scripture memory is one thing they really emphasize.

During this time I had made formal confession of faith in Christ as my Savior and Lord. As most new Christians are, I was pretty fired up and excited about it. My exposure to the Navigators ministry just fueled that fire. One of my favorite aspects of the Navigator adventure was memorizing Scripture. I was pretty good at it (although there were many who were better). There almost seemed to be a culture of challenge that existed there: just how much Scripture could you memorize? Those who carried around the most Scripture memory cards or who had the most stacked on their desk were considered the most spiritual. (I can't say that this was intentionally promoted by the Navigators, but from my point of view for those of us on campus who were involved, there was a sense of spiritual competition).

Well, at the end of my freshman year I went back home to live with my parents for the summer. What I am about to tell you is something I am not proud of. In order to appreciate this you must understand who my parents were and where I came from.

My parents were humble people of Dutch descent. Their parents had come to the United States from the Netherlands. My father was a vegetable farmer. A very strong, quiet, diligent, and faithful Christian. He was a giant of a man and to this day, I have never known someone who worked so hard, so continuously, six days a week. And he was faithful to the Lord. He would faithfully pray and read Scripture every evening after supper. He would make sure we all went to church twice on Sunday. He made sure that my sister and I both went through Christian grade school, high school, and college. But he was quiet, not very outgoing or communicative. Therefore his expressions of faith were usually quite reserved.

My mother passed away when I was five, but I am told she was quite a godly person. My stepmother, whom my father had married when I was seven suffered most of her life with bouts of clinical depression, but there is no question, in spite of her inadequacies, that she was a committed Christian.

Well, being as spiritual as I was, I knew they were not as committed as I, so coming home, I was determined to set them right. I wanted to let them know that they could be so much more. I wanted to shake them out of their doldrums and "exhort" them to become better, more excited Christians. I was both very serious and very sincere.

To this day, I will never get this scene out of my mind and heart. My dad had come home from his usual twelve-hour day, washed up, and was ready for supper. My plan was to confront them with their problem after dinner. So when my dad read Scripture and prayed I thought, "This is the time. Now I will let them know how they are failing as Christians!" So I let them have it: I told them that if they really were Christians that they would be more involved and active. After all, why weren't they involved in a Bible study? Why didn't they evangelize more, go to church more, fellowship more? And of course, if they really wanted to be a dynamic Christian like I was, they would be memorizing Scripture! I let them have it! As I recall my parents had nothing to say; they just listened to me silently.

> I told them that if they really were Christians that they would be more involved and active. After all, why weren't they involved in a Bible study? Why didn't they evangelize more, go to church more, fellowship more? And of course, if they really wanted to be a dynamic Christian like I was, they would be memorizing Scripture!

23

Well, as most college students do, I stayed up late that night, just a little later than my parents. My dad and mom went to bed after the news; I stayed up to watch Johnny Carson. As I was going to my room I passed by theirs and noticed their door was open just a crack. For some reason I peeked in, and what I saw will never get out of my mind. There were my parents, by their bed, on their knees, praying. What they were praying for I of course have no idea. Perhaps they were praying about the chastising their son had just given them. Perhaps they were praying about being better Christians. Perhaps they were praying for the new found excitement their son just displayed and were simply thankful that I had embraced, with all of my misplaced enthusiasm, a real relationship with the Lord. Whatever they were praying, I am sure they were praying for me, because they were faithful, and in the humility of their bedside, I am quite sure they prayed for my sister and me on a daily basis.

But in the moment I saw them praying, I felt like I was hit with a lightning bolt and for the first time in my life (and unfortunately, not the last) I realized that I had a Pharisee in me! This was not an easy realization to absorb, for all my sincerity and enthusiasm were misdirected. I realized that I had seen incidents similar to this before in Scripture.

Luke 18:9-14 portrays a scene that we know well; we just don't usually identify with it. I, however, do identify with it. It is the scene of the Pharisee and the tax collector. In this scene we find two men in the temple praying. One is very proud, verbal, confident, and sure of himself and his spiritual identity. The other is timid, full of self doubt, and perhaps not even sure he should be there. The proud one was the Pharisee; the tentative one was the tax collector.

This scene fits the images that they had within prevalent culture. The Pharisees of course were the well known ones, respected, looked up to, and revered for their spiritual fervor. The tax collectors were looked down upon, despised, often "feared" because of their ability to impose more taxes than were required so that they could keep some on the side, for themselves. Levi (Matthew) had been a tax collector before he joined Jesus.

The Pharisees would be the first to speak; perhaps the first to pray at a temple gathering, or any other gathering. The tax collectors, like this guy, were probably not even seen in the temple, and if they were, I suppose they were in the back of the building. The tax collectors knew I'm sure of the necessity of their occupation, but they also knew how little they were appreciated. Certainly because of abuses, but also because they were in the business of impounding money from the residents. Like our own IRS, they were not exactly honored.

As Scripture says, the Pharisee was "confident" of his own righteousness. This is Problem #1 and reveals the double edged sword of our faith. Certainly we want people to be confident of their faith and assured of their salvation. Most definitely we want people to be passionate Christians. But the problem was that this Pharisee was confident of "his" own righteousness. As Christians we are confident not in *"our"* righteousness, but the righteousness that is found in Christ!

> All I know is that on that day, I was the Pharisee. I was confident of my own righteousness. I was so spiritual, and thought my parents weren't.

There is a line that we cross somewhere (I will reveal how this happens in chapter 4) where in the midst of our own pursuit of godliness we find ourselves being righteous, holy and spiritual. We know that what we are doing is 'right' and holy and good, and we want others to be that way too. And so we display our spirituality as "examples" for others to follow, and along the way perhaps even "exhort" others who aren't where we are—spiritually speaking.

All I know is that on that day, I was the Pharisee. I was confident of my own righteousness. I was so spiritual, and thought my parents weren't. In a way, I was thanking God that I was not like them...I was pounding my chest and pointing out my own spiritual superiority.

My parents, on the other hand, reminded me of the tax collector. Humbly listening to their Pharisee son and then going to God, on their knees, at night, where nobody could see—except their snooping son. Let me tell you, there is nothing so devastating as being hit with the reality of your own pharisaicalism, and it is most revealing in the face of true humility. Humility outranks Pharisaicalism and self-righteousness every time. As Jesus said, "I tell you that this man [the tax collector], rather than the other went home justified before God. For everyone who exalts himself will be humbled, and he who humbles himself will be exalted" (Luke 18:14).

Pharisaical Moments

Who can say that they have not had pharisaical moments? In today's world which would you choose: to be in the limelight, admired for your spiritual prowess, seen as a godly man (or woman), a great pray-er, sought after for your wisdom, and given favored places within your own spiritual realm; or someone who was quiet, not sure of himself, questioning your own sense of *spiritualness* and acceptability, and not looked upon as a godly person? Certainly we are not supposed to strive to be like the tax collector, are we?

I'm not sure how to answer this question. It haunts me. I know people who try to portray a humble spirituality, and some who even pull it off. But I am convinced that this tax collector wasn't trying to be humble...he just was. Are we supposed to have a spiritual inferiority complex? Well, honestly I don't

> Who can say that they have not had pharisaical moments?

think that is quite right either. Lewis Smedes describes facing a similar reality:

> The boy inside me was a frightened little Pharisee, chasing the carrot of divine approval at the end of an endless stick...So, what can you do, what can you do except knock yourself out chasing all those

26

wonderful virtues, faking it too often, now and then downgrading yourself so you would at least get credit for honesty, but always trying your darndest to be good enough, and ending up with a mountain of misery on your back because you knew you were not, never would be good enough.[1]

I know that Paul must have struggled with his own sinfulness. After he was taken out of his Pharisaical culture (Paul, as Saul, had been a Pharisee) he faced his sinfulness for what it really was. The seventh chapter of Romans reveals a struggle: " I do not understand what I do. For what I want to do I do not do, but what I hate I do…For what I do is not the good I want to do; no, the evil I do not what to do—this I keep doing" (Rom. 7:15, 19)

We know he concludes with an answer. An answer that has nothing to do with his own spirituality, with his own ability to keep the law, nor his own ability to be godly and stay away from his sinful impulses. This Scripture even seems to imply that he struggled with a sin that he "keep(s) doing". We don't normally see this part of the verse. We see a sin that he walked away from. After all, to be godly, don't you have to confess your sin, and then not do it anymore? Certainly this is the standard that we hold for those in leadership. But if I can press this point a little, what about this consideration: Is it possible that Paul struggled with some kind of addiction? "…the evil I do not want to do—this I keep doing." Hmm…it sure doesn't sound like someone who has "conquered" or has "victory" over his sin problem!

He concluded, of course, that the victory was not his, but Christ's. He concluded that the solution wasn't about the reality of his own sinfulness but the reality of Christ's work already completed: "Thanks be to God—through Jesus Christ our Lord!...Therefore, there is now no condemnation for those who are in Christ Jesus, because through Christ Jesus the law of the Spirit of life set me free from the law of sin and death" (Rom. 7:25, 8:1, 2).

The Pharisee style is to find out what the problem or sin is, and to fix it by coming up with a method or system of overcoming

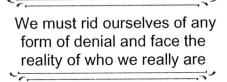

We must rid ourselves of any form of denial and face the reality of who we really are

that sin so that they would no longer "do" it. The Christ-way, which is the way that Paul discovered here, was not that he could overcome his sinfulness with righteousness, but that in his sinfulness, or to say it another way, that in spite of himself and his sinfulness, he was *in* Christ. He wore Christ's righteousness. Jesus Christ *is* our righteousness, and there is nothing we can add to that, not even after our salvation. This is very similar to what Dallas Willard in his book *The Divine Conspiracy* calls "the gospel of sin management." We will talk about this more in chapter six under the section, "The Not Enough Syndrome". Basically, it is the idea that the Christian life is all about managing sin. But let me say this: if that is what the Christian life is all about, we would work overtime, twenty-four/seven, and still be unable to manage our sin. It's a false delusion to think that we can. What's more is that if we spent all our hours trying to manage sin, we would not have time for anything else, which of course, is exactly where the Pharisees were at.

Knowing who we are—honestly—is the key to transformation. We must rid ourselves of any form of denial and face the reality of who we really are. That's what I suggest Paul was doing in this passage. Let's put aside the delusion of any kind of self-produced holiness. My friend John Fischer makes this clear in his book, *12 Steps of a Recovering Pharisee (like me)*. He likens being a Pharisee to a 12-step program. The first step is to recognize and "own" your own Pharisaical tendencies. He says in his introduction:

> This is the gospel for those courageous enough to tear off their masks of adequacy and self-righteousness and get on with a

life of gratitude and love for others. This is
the Pharisee recovery group of which I
speak, and these are the steps that will lead
us out. I know, for I am an expert in the
downturned look, the haughty eye, the
wagging head—and I've   had   enough
of it. Welcome to the group.[2]

The Pharisee in You

The question is, can you find *"The Pharisee In Me"*?
What kind of probing do you have to do and introspection do
you need to resort to in order to find times when you were
self-righteous, judgmental, and Pharisaical? Do you, like
me, have images and scenes from your past that haunt you?
The ability to do this, to locate in our memory banks times
we have been Pharisaical is not only cathartic, it is healing,
transforming, and empowering. We then are able to put
ourselves in the same boat as everyone else: sinners who
need a Savior, sinners who are incapable of our own
righteousness and holiness.

Many years ago, I was on staff in a church in
Michigan. I was young, and quite frankly still trying to find
myself, and because of that, I was insecure. The senior
pastor of that church was, although much older than I,
equally insecure. While the details are not important, let's
just say that he had a history of not doing well leading staff
ministries, and I knew it. Knowing this didn't really help me
in my relationship with him. Although I was half his age, I
looked down on him and wasn't willing to work out our
differences. Yes, I had a Pharisaical attitude toward him. I
had a *Pharisee In Me*. Although I left that church for another
and severed our relationship, I will never forget him. I was
the Pharisee saying, "I thank you Lord that I am not like him."
Years later, I realized one important thing about him;
although insecure, he was a faithful servant trying his best to
please the Lord with the gifts God had given him. Through
this realization, and although he did not know it, whenever I
thought of him, I would say a little prayer thanking God for

him and asking God to bless him in whatever he was doing—the even better thing would be for me to call him and ask his forgiveness for my superior attitude and lack of humility. Sadly, I never did this.

Perhaps you have felt no association with the Pharisees, and have early on concluded that they were a bad sort, certainly not someone like you. Anytime we portray any sense of self-righteousness, legalism, and pharisaicalism we take on the Pharisaical garb; and we need to face this reality for what it is. This chapter is for you and my hope is that it has helped you confront the *"Pharisee in Me"*...that is, in YOU. However, if there is still some lingering sense of denial on your part I want to show you perhaps for the first time, how easy it is to be a Pharisee. It happens to us without notice; within a syndrome I call "The Pharisaical Lure". This is the subject we will turn to next.

Chapter 4

The Pharisaical Lure ·

"Be on your guard against the yeast of the Pharisees."
Matthew 16:6

When you read Matthew 16:5-12 you are confronted with the concept of the "yeast of the Pharisees." This is *the* key verse for this study! I hope you memorize it. If you have purchased the study materials you will have received a *Pharisee Prevention Handbook* and a *Pharisee In Me* card, both of which emphasize this verse.

Yeast and Denial

This Scripture is significant in that it gives us insight into the draw and attraction of what I call "The Pharisaical Lure". I hope that if you are in a study group you will wrestle with the significance of yeast. What are its properties and characteristics? And more importantly, what was Jesus referring to

> Something compels us to want to be above, better, or more spiritual than others

when he used the metaphor of yeast?

Like a fishing lure or magnet, there is something so irresistible that it pulls us into a Pharisaical attitude. Something compels us to want to be above, better, or more spiritual than others. While being a Pharisee is repugnant to us, it is at the same time irresistible. More importantly, it is something that captures us unaware. Someone asked me, "Did the Pharisees know that they were being 'pharisaical'" (that is, self-righteous)? My personal assessment is that they were in denial. They were so caught up in being holy and spiritual that they were not aware of their judgmental spirit or sin of superiority. Stephen Arterburn and Jack Felton, in their book, *Toxic Faith*, make this comment on the subtleties of the infusion of self-righteousness into our lives:

> In the early stages, it is difficult to identify when religion becomes addiction. It looks so good....They escape into an unreal world where people, ideas, and rules replace a relationship with God....Religious addiction doesn't occur overnight. It is a long progression that subtly captures every aspect of the addict's life. [1]

Denial and yeast are two ingredients which contribute to a kind of Pharisaical 'take-over' within us. Rather than give you the "answer" to the question of yeast, I will pass on that issue and let you struggle with it within your study group.

> We don't know we are Pharisees because we don't understand how we can become something that we detest.

If you want to, however, go to the endnotes and consider the power of yeast.[2] However, I do want to say a word about denial.

Denial is something we all fall into from time to time. Denial is common. We can be "in denial" for small things, like not admitting that you snore at night, or something more serious, like an addiction of some kind. Facing our denial is the first part of seeing our tendency toward self-righteousness and legalism. This is precisely how John Fischer approaches this topic in his book. Pointing to Matthew 6:23, he says, "A blind person knows he is blind. A Pharisee thinks he can see, and this is why the "light" within him is actually darkness. Jesus called the Pharisees "blind guides.""[3] John then proceeds to write this book from the perspective of a person going to an AA meeting, a person dealing with an addiction. The first aspect of this is denial, owning up to who we really are.

We don't know we are Pharisees because we don't understand how we can become something that we detest. We think we are understanding, when in reality we may be judgmental. We think we are full of grace and forgiveness, when in reality we want a little vengeance. We think we are humble, when in reality our humility isn't genuine. We think we believe in salvation though Christ alone through his grace alone, when in reality we really want rules and works to govern our life and the lives of those we come in contact with. In short, we think we are not Pharisees when in reality we are. This is the great deception...this is self-denial at its best.

There is a book that I very much like called "Leadership and Self-Deception" and although it is not a "Christian" book, its truth and ability to get to the core issue of denial is profound. Its contention is that the reason that leaders of organizations don't lead very well and that organizations are unable to rid themselves of certain problems is that the leaders themselves are part of the problem, and they are in denial about it: "Identify someone with a problem and you'll be identifying someone who resists the suggestion that he has a problem. That's self-deception—the inability to see that one has a problem."[4] Specifically, regarding organizations they point out, "...self-deception is a particularly difficult sort of problem. To the extent organizations are beset with self-deception—and most of them are—they can't see the problem. Most organizations are stuck in the box."[5] Their meaning here is that when you are self-deceived and in denial, you are stuck in a box of perception. All you can see is your perspective of things, creating a "box" around yourself which defines your own reality. You (and organizations, including churches) are sure you are right, because all you can see are things from your own frame of reference.

But rather than prolong this concept, I want to show you how we are drawn unknowingly and unwittingly into a life of self-righteousness, legalism, and judgementalism. It is precisely because we aren't aware of how this happens to us that we are in denial. Coming to grips with this can take us out of our denial and allow us to see things as they really are. It is a syndrome or model of what I call the Pharisaical Lure.

Please review the model below and then follow along with how we are pulled into a Pharisaical attitude almost without notice.

The Pharisaical Lure

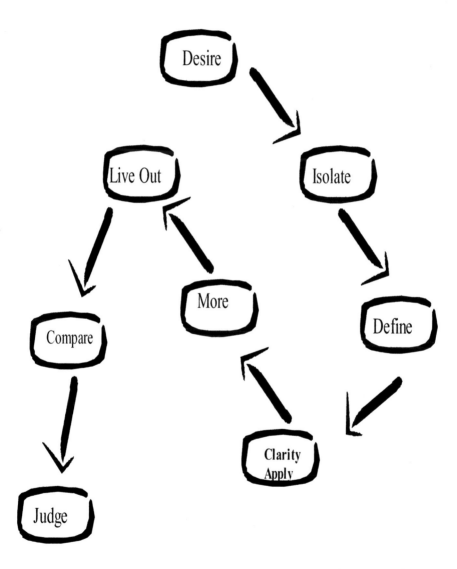

We start with the most innocent, sincere, and right intentions. We start with a sincere DESIRE. Our desire and intention is to honor God, to be obedient, and to do what he

tells us in His Word. We desire to honor and glorify God.
Virtually every Christian I know starts from this premise: they
want to please
God, they want to honor Him, they want to be godly,
obedient, and they want to be good Christians. They want to
be spiritual. To put it another way, I don't know of any
Christian who doesn't want to please God. If you
immediately thought of someone you know who you doubt
regarding that being their motivating force you may have just
had a Pharisaical moment.

What comes out of this desire to be obedient to God
is to ISOLATE a portion of Scripture or a command. Since
there is a lot that is contained in Scripture it can be a bit
overwhelming, so we naturally want to break it down into
manageable pieces. We take a portion of Scripture, isolate it
(from the rest of Scripture...and often from its context), and
then we try to figure out what it says. This is natural and
normal. We don't know how to "do" Galatians; rather, as a
classic example, we will isolate the "fruit of the spirit"
passage in Galatians 5:22, 23 and look at it closer so we can
understand it's meaning.

After picking out a portion of Scripture, we then try to
DEFINE it. We want to understand what it is God is saying
to us. What does He mean in this part of the Word? And so,
we try to define what the fruit of the spirit are. What does
God mean when he says we are to have love, joy, peace,
patience, kindness, etc? We take it and try to elaborate
further on what it is supposed to mean.

This leads us to the next step which is critical, and the
one we are most interested in. We want to gain CLARITY.
When we have clarity we can then APPLY it. We want to
know what it clearly means and how it applies to our
everyday life. The goal is to apply it, and in order to apply it
we need to know what it really means. Before I can "do" it, I
need to know how it applies to my life. This, of course, is
consistent with our desire to please and be obedient to God.

We don't stop there, however; we now want
MORE...more specifics about how to apply it to our life.
Forget generalities, we really want to live this stuff out! So,

we look for specific ways to apply it to our particular life. For example: "I will pray every morning for thirty minutes"; or I will try to be more joyful...and here's how: I will smile even if I am feeling low. If the fruit of the spirit is joy, then I must find a way to be joyful. As a good Christian I must be joyful, so I will practice joyfulness by smiling a lot. I will tell people I'm happy, content, and joyful. This is what I will work on and how I will apply it to my life.

Of course, then we try to LIVE it OUT. Our goal is to be "doers of the word, and not merely hearers" (ref. Ja.1:22, 23)! We take our clearly defined application we've decided to work on and begin doing it. Then, after awhile, we begin to develop a habit. Perhaps after a week, a month, six months, or a year after concentrating on doing this particular thing we actually become pretty good at it. We are good at praying or being joyful or memorizing Scripture. We've applied the "discipline" to incorporate it into our lives and now we're experts at it.

Quite frankly, we don't even have to be that good at it. All we need is to be assured or "convicted" that this is something we "should" be doing. This is often the case after a weekend seminar or a week-long retreat. We've been saturated in a particular concept and we come down from the mountain all hyped up about whatever it is we learned. Whether it is prayer, Scripture memory, worship, evangelism, a particular "path to victorious Christian living," or whatever the topic may have been, we are sure that this is something everyone else "should" be doing. We become crusaders for "the cause." So even before we are really good at it, our convictions alone compensate for our not yet being good at something we are sure to get good at. We announce our commitments and suggest that others follow.

Up until now, it is all well and good, but now we begin to turn a corner. As we become pretty good at this one thing, we look around and notice that others aren't quite as good at it as we are. And we begin to COMPARE. It's natural, it happens. Show me someone who doesn't compare and I will show you someone who is in denial. We all compare. It's right at this point that the Pharisaical Lure has us trapped, which you will see in a moment.

> As we become pretty good at this one thing, we look around and notice that others aren't quite as good at it as we are.

Comparing is something we are sure we don't do. This is an area of denial as I mentioned above. We know it is wrong to compare, so we are pretty sure we don't do it. It's kind of like a psychological self-talk we do with ourselves. "No I'm not comparing, I'm trying to set an example," is the way the thought usually goes. But comparing by any other name is still comparing.

Think about it, it's built into our communication system. For someone to be tall, someone has to be small…or at least "average" height. If I say, "I am full" at dinner time, then I am quite naturally comparing that to being hungry. In school we have a built in comparative system. If someone is an "A" student that person is automatically deemed intelligent, bright, smart, and on top of things, compared with a "C" student who would be considered "average" in my day or below average in these days. An average student would be considered mediocre, perhaps an underachiever, and probably not destined for greatness….not someone we would follow…not a leader.

Comparing is the natural progression of what we do because it also validates what we do. We want to know that what we do is the correct way of doing things and so our sense of comparing seems to validate our spiritual maturity. If I pray more, better, more dramatically than the next person than I must be more spiritual. If I bring into the fold more people through my evangelistic efforts than I must be a pretty "effective" Christian—compared to others. If I go to more Bible studies, or every time the church door opens and I am there, then I must be a spiritual giant that others should look up to.

We compare not only ourselves to others, but others to others. Within our evangelical circles we do this to see who we want to follow or be like or hang out with. I have known people, for example, whom I would call "natural lovers". That is, they possess a nurturing gift that causes them to care for and help others. It comes to them naturally. So when you look at the "gifts of the spirit" (Gal. 5) and you see "love" is at the top of the list you want to know how to "do" love. Well, regarding the people I am talking about, they possess a natural gift of love but I have witnessed a "comparing to" among certain fellowships. "Why don't you be like so and so, look at what they do" would be a typical comment. Who are they being compared to? Those that don't possess the gift—perhaps someone who is more cerebral, more of a thinking person. Is he or she any less spiritual because they don't "love" as much as the other person? Certainly, these are the implications that come from comparing. And of course we know that the Pharisees were really good at this. And so are the modern day Pharisees...you and I.

You see, in one millisecond, or in a "New York minute", after we compare, we begin to JUDGE. And there you have it. We are now Pharisees. What started as a sincere and innocent desire ended up as full blown self-righteousness! Comparing almost always results in judging, especially within the Christian community.

Judging comes when we determine based on either the comparison of our actions to another; or based upon the comparison of others to others; or based upon our convictions which have come out of our study (or a recent retreat) of a particular aspect of Scripture. In comparison, others are not as spiritual, or mature or holy or convicted or "right" as we are. Our judging is usually what we think of as "light judging". What I mean by this is that we don't "judge" based upon a person's salvation, but on a person's actions (or lack of them). Rarely (although it does occur) do we question a person's salvation; rather, we question their *degree* of spirituality, or holiness, or obedience. In other words, we question a person's "righteousness".

A common reaction to this will be: you will go to the Scriptures that refer to "accountability" or "by their fruits you will know them" and conclude that what I am saying is bogus because the Bible says we are to hold others accountable and we are to "judge" someone's degree of Christianity by their fruits. Armed with Scriptures like these we feel pretty justified for pointing out someone's short comings or "nailing someone to the wall." I will talk a little more about this in Chapter Eight on *Dismantling Pharisaical Mind-Sets*. But for now let me say that the purpose of this chapter is to point out how the natural progression or syndrome of the Pharisaical Lure works.

To see further how this works, I would like to take an example and run it though the cycle of the Pharisaical Lure. If you are studying this with a group in the study guide I have suggested that you take Matthew 12:1-8 and discuss how the desire to honor the command "you shall not work on the Sabbath day…" succumbed to the syndrome and became a Pharisaical and self-righteous law which was ultimately used by the Pharisees to judge others. So I will not deal with that issue and hope that your group does this together.

I gave you an indication of how the syndrome or *Pharisaical Lure* works with the issue of prayer, and even the issue of "loving" as the first on the list of the fruit of the spirit. As a further example, I want to take the issue of Scripture memory—the one I struggled with regarding my parents, to demonstrate the Pharisaical Lure in action.

Pharisaical Lure in action

First I start with a sincere DESIRE to please, honor, and be obedient to God's Word. I want to "do" what His Word says, and honor Him with my obedience. This is where we all start. We all want to honor and please Him.

So I ISOLATE a portion of Scripture to begin to dissect it so that I can understand what God is saying. In this particular case I have come to Psalm 119:11: "I have hidden your word in my heart that I might not sin against you." OKAY, so we ask ourselves, "What does God mean here regarding hiding his Word in my heart?" "What is it that God wants me to do to hide the word in my heart?" A natural conclusion is Scripture memory. We conclude that this is what David was talking about and what he did to combat sin in his life. Now, you memorize Scripture to reduce the amount of sin in your life. This is just another case of sin management, of trying not to sin.

The next step is to gain more CLARITY so that we can APPLY it to our lives. We know that God through David said to hide His Word in his heart and we have concluded that that means Scripture memory. So now I set out to do just that. The verse clearly teaches Scripture memory.

So, we want MORE specifics. Exactly how am I supposed to do this? We create a design or action steps to "do" this stuff. We want to apply it in concrete fashion. So now, I determine, "I will memorize one verse per day, or one per week," "I will use Scripture memory cards (AKA: the Navigators) so that I can take them with me and review them on an on-going basis." I will find a memory partner and recite them to this person once a week so that I can keep myself sharp" etc. For example, I have known of people who have set out to memorize the entire book of Proverbs. Memorize, memorize, memorize! All in a quest to "live out specifically" what God has said in His word!

Now, all I do is simply LIVE it OUT. I begin to develop a practice or habit. I do this religiously every day or every week. I practice and review often. I use my spare moments during the day to go through my memory cards. And now after a few months of doing this, my card stack begins to mount up. I have quite a list of Scriptures which I have memorized; perhaps my stack is too big to carry around so now I just carry with me part of my stack—maybe just this month's verses. The result: I have gotten pretty good at doing this. I'm a Scripture memory pro! Who can compare to my mastery of the Word?

And yes, now I begin to COMPARE. I look around and wonder why more people aren't memorizing Scripture like I am. Why aren't they quoting Scripture like I am? If I am in a group or fellowship that emphasizes Scripture memory I might even look around to see how big their stack of memory cards is. How many Scriptures have they memorized?

And now, I am beginning to JUDGE others regarding their Scripture memory practices (or lack thereof). I might think (or say), "They just give their own opinions, and they don't quote Scripture when they talk". They don't know the Word enough because they aren't memorizing Scripture. (We will talk about "the not enough syndrome" in a chapter six).

We are now implying that these people (whoever they may be) aren't as spiritual, holy or obedient as I am because they are not memorizing Scripture (or not memorizing "enough"). I have judged their degree of spirituality based upon my own particular competency of memorizing Scripture. I have taken a portion of God's Word and applied it in such a way that I've made it into a legalistic standard. Others now have to memorize Scripture like I do or they're not quite as spiritual as I am.

> We don't question a person's salvation—what we do is judge their spiritual maturity or vibrancy. We judge their *degree* of spirituality

Do you see how easy this is and how we fall into the trap? This is why I call it a lure. We start with a good thing, memorizing Scripture—and don't get me wrong here, it is a good thing—and we end up comparing and judging others because they aren't memorizing Scripture like we are.

Once again, we don't question a person's salvation—what we do is judge their spiritual maturity or vibrancy. We judge their *degree* of spirituality. This person is a good Christian; this one is marginal.

And now, let's tie together the concept of the "yeast" and the Pharisaical Lure. The Pharisaical Lure operates just like yeast. Like yeast it takes over our entire existence as a Christian. It infiltrates and dominates our entire being and operates our comparative nature. It takes over and whatever our issue is, whatever our specialty or our area of interest, it becomes "*our thing*", our focus. We make it something that becomes to us *"the"* thing. So *"our thing"* becomes *"the"* thing and we are sure everyone else must make it *"their thing"* as well or they are not being obedient— at least, not as obedient as we are!

The Pharisaical Lure works itself out in many forms and takes many shapes. There are, after all, many types of Pharisees, displaying many aspects of self-righteousness, legalism, and judgementalism. Looking at the Pharisaical Lure and at Pharisees from many angles, will make us more aware of their presence in our midst; maybe even in our own lives! This is what we will turn to next.

Chapter 5

Seven Types of Pharisees
The Pharisaical Lure Continued

"Everything they do is done for men to see..."
Matthew. 23:5

This section is adapted from William Barclay's commentary, "The Daily Study Bible, Gospel of Matthew, The Westminster Press, Philadelphia, 1975. I am indebted to Barclay for the basic concept and titles attributed to the seven types of Pharisees and have tried to expand and identify them in our everyday world.

Apparently even the Jews began to identify and recognize different types of Pharisees. Different characteristics that epitomize one kind of Pharisee from another. They were all Pharisees; they just presented themselves differently.

These characterizations I will also take up in a little different way in Chapter Seven, *Warning Signs and Dangers of the Pharisaical Lure; Seven Tendencies and Traits*. They are taken from Matthew 23: 13-32 and Luke 11:37-54. In your study guide you will be encouraged to read and discuss these.

The purpose here is to broaden the field and definition of what it means to be a Pharisee. We may have had certain ideas of who and what Pharisees were and who they are today. In comparing your concept of pharisaicalism you may have prematurely eliminated yourself from the possibility of being a Pharisee. Perhaps this chapter will bring this subject closer to home. Perhaps some of these characteristics are yours as well. If we have not nailed it down in this chapter, by the 7th chapter we should have included enough similarities for you to see the "Pharisee In Me"—that is, in YOU.

The Shoulder Pharisee

The first type of Pharisee described by Barclay is the *Shoulder Pharisee.* He was the one who patted himself on the back and let everyone know just how good he was. We have lot of Shoulder Pharisees around; they are just subtle and smooth in the way that they go about patting themselves on the back.

The trick, you see, is to do it in a way that actually provides opportunity for others to pat you on the back. Describing in detail some good thing that you did is one way to get some patting on the back. For example, let's say if someone decided to give a meal to someone in the church and told you the story of how she went through all kinds of conniptions to get the meal pulled together. Perhaps she went to three different grocery stores to get just the right ingredients. Then in the midst of picking up the kids from school, and preparing the meal for her family, she slaved over a hot oven to get the meal for the family receiving the meal. Then, so that they would receive the meal hot, she ran it over (actually more likely drove across town) so that they could have the meal just in time for dinner, followed by her rushing back home to give her family their meal, which by now may be cold. This is just one small example of how we can dramatize a story of a good thing we did so that the hearer of the story will pause to think how great a servant for Christ you are. Lewis Smedes calls this "attacks of virtue;"

45

The dumbest heresy ever circulated among the elect is that virtue is its own reward. I can confide to you that I have personally survived several severe attacks of virtue...what most of us lusters after virtue want is not to be virtuous but to have reputations thereof... we are deadly afraid that someone might see our flaws and discover we are frauds....Lust for virtue is the denial of grace in our lives. And the denial of grace is the most fatal of all joy killers.[1]

Wait-a-little Pharisee

Then there is the *Wait-a-little Pharisee*. This is someone who may come up with all kinds of excuses for not doing something good because what they are doing is more spiritual. If you have watched my video, or heard me speak, you will recall the story of the guy so busy reading his Bible he didn't have time to fellowship and be social with a group of Christians at a pool party.

> Is it possible to be too spiritual? Is it possible to be too holy or too perfect?

I once belonged to a church which focused on small group ministry as the way to "do church." One of the things that this ministry emphasized was fellowship, eating meals together and enjoying each other's company. This is a good thing. Well, one day, we were having a pool party and we all gathered at a friend's house to share in a pot-luck and swim in their pool and simply have a good time. During the majority of this time, there was a man who was in a corner reading his Bible. This wasn't some kind of urgent search for an answer to a problem in God's Word; rather, this was normal for him.

46

While other people were enjoying each other's company and fellowshipping together, he was reading the Scriptures; which we all know has to be more spiritual than fellowship, right?

I've often asked the question, sometimes with a bit of puzzlement in people's faces, "Is it possible to be too spiritual?" Is it possible to be too holy or too perfect? Is it even possible to sin while reading the Bible? These are some of the questions that you should wrestle with if you are going through this in a study or home group.

If it is possible to be too spiritual, what are the circumstances surrounding the situation? For example, in the case above with the guy reading the Bible, he projected an attitude of, "Hey, don't bother me with trivial stuff! I'm over here reading the Word! Can't you see?" I believe that in cases like this there is sin involved, a sin of super-spiritual righteousness on display for others to see; while neglecting the simple act of being with and loving those who are in our fellowship. We are to be a part of a body of Christ, a supportive group of believers who have come together to build up, encourage, and help each other. To read the Word all by yourself, in a corner, while others are interacting, is rude at best and too spiritual. After all, you can't be doers of the Word if you're always reading the Word.

There is something that makes me uptight in the presence of someone who "has it all together." Maybe it's just me, but I feel terribly "dirty," "sinful," and "inadequate" when I'm around someone who seems so perfect and so holy. Quite frankly, it gives me the creeps. One thing I know for sure is that I can't measure up to their constant display of spiritual appropriateness. They're always doing the right thing, saying the right words, praying the right prayers, recalling the right Scriptures, serving, serving, serving; all the while, here I am, a bumbling human with a roller coaster life who loves the Lord, but doesn't seen quite so spiritual. How about you: do you look up to those who have it all together with respect, or do you feel somehow dirty in the presence of perfection? The wait-a-little Pharisee is always doing things that are spiritually appropriate, things you can see; but do they see me and do they see you? Are they real? Do they live a real life? Can they really identify with and accept you and me with all our peculiarities and short comings...or are they better than we are?

Bruised Pharisee

Then you have the *Bruised Pharisee,* who in his quest for purity wouldn't allow himself to look at a woman for fear of lusting. Consequently, he would bump into things causing him to be bruised. I imagine these bruises were his badges of honor, announcing to everyone who saw him just how holy and spotless he was. It's hard to imagine looking down when women were around—running into walls, carts, poles, and perhaps other people in my quest to avoid lusting. But today, we have people who are convinced that TV is the tool of the devil and do not watch it for fear of seeing some woman in slinky garb who would cause them to lust.

Admittedly, it is becoming harder to avoid these things. But we would have to avoid reading major magazines because they have racy ads or avoid driving down the highway because of sexually implicit billboards that line the streets. We would almost never be able to see a quality motion picture because of some of the scenes that are contained in them, even if they are short and in passing. Quite frankly, these days it's virtually impossible to avoid lustful scenes and to do so we would almost have to remove ourselves from the world and confine ourselves to a monastery. Of course, we would then be known for our spirituality because of our avoidance of the world (look for more on this in my resource on *"How to Lose the World without Really Trying!"*). Under such scenarios we try to equate spirituality with avoidance, and our abstinence becomes badges of holiness so others will notice, or so we won't become contaminated. Avoidance and abstinence become our "bruises" in pursuit of a sinless, holy and pure life.

In the case of the *Bruised Pharisee*, shutting your eyes is equivalent to not going out into the world, never being where the world is. As John Fischer adds,

> Many evangelicals mistakenly believe that a person's spirituality and closeness to God are inversely proportionate to the amount of sin in that person's life. More sin, less of God; more of God, less sin, the ultimate goal being sinlessness--a state that no one we know has actually achieved, but is theoretically plausible nonetheless....This equation is carefully bolstered by glowing testimonies and the close-to-perfect reputations of those who are close to God. Ministers and those in "full-time Christian service" are closer than anybody and thus the furthest from sin.[2]

The fallacy is that if I can just shut my eyes long enough, or if I can immerse myself and every waking moment within the church, I might be able to avoid the sin of the world, and therefore avoid sinning.

But this is not a one plus one equation. Nor does one good deed subtract one sinful act. Neither is it a diet, where the avoidance of carbs will allow me to lose weight. Keeping the law and avoidance of the world does not add up; but the Pharisees thought it did. Commenting on the pursuit of perfection in keeping the law (and keeping away from "the world") Bob George says, "The reason that the law is useless for producing the life that God desires is that it deals only with externals....If merely shaping up our actions were what God desired, then the Pharisees would have been His favorites." [3]

Hump-back Pharisee

Barclay then mentions the *Hump-Back Pharisee*. This is the guy who wanted others to see how humble he was, so he would walk hunched over. He would apparently have a walk of humility, dragging his feet along the path so others could admire his sense of unworthiness.

You may not know anyone who demonstrates their humility in such a way, but I am sure you can think of instances when you knew of someone (not yourself of course) who seemed to pronounce their humility in such a way that all could see. What about the wealthy Christian who drives an old beat up car, when in reality he could afford any car he wishes. His choice of the old car is to demonstrate to others that he's not concerned about *things*…after all, those are just worldly treasures. But the old car is really his badge of humility, his method for demonstrating his spirituality.

Perhaps you know of someone who doesn't do something because they are "unworthy"…which of course, is really good spiritual talk. A few years ago, I was in a home group, and it was prayer time. The guys were in one room and the women in another room. I was sitting on the floor while most of the guys were sitting on couches and chairs so I already had put myself in a lowly position. Although I really can't remember what the topic or issue was I do remember saying that "I didn't feel worthy." Just that second, my friend dropped down to the floor from the coach and put his head sideways on the floor to show that he could get lower than me…therefore he could "out humble me." Apparently, whatever the issue was, I came off as trying to demonstrate my humility. I am, after all, a Pharisee, not knowing sometimes of my own tendencies toward self-righteousness.

Remember all those "Beatitudes" in Matthew 5? You know, blessed be the "poor in spirit", the "meek", the "poor in heart", etc.? We seem to think that these are indicators on how we can become humble, meek, and poor in heart, that this is our quest, that this is how we should act. However, as Dallas Willard so aptly points out, "The Beatitudes simply cannot be "good news" if they are understood as a set of "how tos" for achieving blessedness. They would then only amount to a new legalism. They would not serve to throw open the kingdom—anything but. They would impose a new brand of Phariseeism, a new way of closing the door—as well as some very gratifying new possibilities for the human engineering of righteousness."[4] I couldn't have said it better! My unworthiness doesn't make me humble; all it does is acknowledge that I'm unworthy. Humility doesn't make me more worthy, either.

Compounding Pharisee

Then there was the *Compounding Pharisee*. This is the guy who felt that his good deeds compounded over time, accruing with "interest". He felt his deeds added together had some kind of overwhelming leverage over God. This is the Shoulder Pharisee times ten! He is a guy who feels that God ought to be glad to have him on board. What would God do without him? God certainly must be grateful for all this guy has done.

I wonder sometimes if there is any correspondence to this and the concept of having many crowns. Within some evangelical circles there is an emphasis regarding how many crowns you will have when you get to heaven. This suggests some sort of hierarchy in heaven—the more crowns you accumulate here on earth, the better the place you will occupy in heaven. Ideas of the "crown" concept come from Scriptures such as 2 Timothy 4:8, "Now there is in store for me the crown of righteousness, which the Lord, the righteous Judge, will award to me on that day—and not only to me, but also to all who have longed for his appearing." But the idea that is often promoted is that there are many crowns which we can receive as a result of our works or efforts, the crown of righteousness being just one. There is the victorious crown, the crown of glory, the crown of life, the crown of righteousness, etc. That these "crowns" are

> The presumption being that God is into quantity. More effort, more reward—more crowns. Less effort, less of a reward

51

rewards seems to allude that they are achieved, the result of our effort and spiritual success.

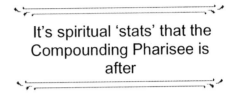

It's spiritual 'stats' that the Compounding Pharisee is after

But whatever will happen in heaven, the thought here is that the more you do, the better you are, the presumption being that God is into quantity. More effort, more reward—more crowns. Less effort, less of a reward. And the rewards come as a result of "spiritual" effectiveness, not everyday living. "Spiritual" activities result in crowns; nothing else matters. And so now, in the process of achieving our rewards and adding up our crowns, we split life into two segments: one sacred or spiritual—this is the one that counts; and the other secular, where our everyday life is lived out in work and home—this is not as important as those "spiritual" things—or so the thinking goes. Once again, maybe this is indicative of the person who is always at the church whenever the church doors are open. They are adding up their crowns here on earth so that they can cash them in when they get to heaven.

Perhaps they have shown you their collection of spiritual trophies that they've accumulated here on earth so that both you and God can admire their good work. Perhaps you've even seen or head of their spiritual credentials in your church: brought twenty people to the Lord, went on six short term missions trips, sings in the choir, feeds the poor at the homeless shelter, still married to the same woman, family members all fall perfectly in line, all of his kids are involved in ministry, and on and on it goes.

Sometimes the compounding concept inhabits women who suffer from the Proverbs 31 trap. They read all that that woman did, and set out to be like her...so that they can be the spiritual super-woman they were designed to be. Maybe they've even made a list, and then proceeded to exhaust themselves trying to fill all the qualifications that the Proverbs 31 woman did. Along the way, they are compounding their points and adding up their crowns. Never mind that the Proverbs 31 woman was most likely a composite picture of what a godly woman does. Or perhaps they are more like Martha, always serving so that others would see, and never really sitting at Jesus feet. Just so everyone sees them serve, that's all that counts.

It's spiritual 'stats' that the Compounding Pharisee is after. Like a spiritual baseball player they want the most RBI's or the highest batting average; like a spiritual football player, they want most completions or highest quarterback rating; like a spiritual collegiate athlete, they want to be drafted in the first round, and if possible, be the first pick. Compounding Pharisees need to heed Paul's warning in Galatians 3:3: "Are you so foolish? After beginning with the Spirit, are you now trying to attain your goal by human effort?" As I study Scripture, what I see is not that we have many crowns, but one crown. And it is not a crown earned by our own efforts toward spirituality, but given to us by God's grace. And in the end, we lay our crowns before Him, who is seated on the throne, just as we sing: "Crown Him with many crowns, the Lamb before His throne…", and as Revelation sets the scene: "…the twenty-four elders fall down before him who sits on the throne, and worship him who lives for ever and ever. They lay their crowns before the throne and say: 'You are worthy, our Lord and God, to receive glory and honor and power, for you created all things, and by your will they were created and have their being.'" And as we peek into the discovery of the Lord of Lords we see: "His eyes are like blazing fire, and on his head are many crowns." (Rev. 19:12). The crowns are His, and we are His crowns! Who are "we," "…all who long for his appearing" (2 Tim. 4:8). Who longs for His appearing? All who love Him, who live their life for Him! If you are a Christian, if you love the Lord, then that includes you!

Fearing Pharisee

Next, there is the *Fearing Pharisee*. He did good deeds out of fear of judgment. He was insecure and never quite sure if he was doing "enough" for

God. This is a guy who apparently knew he was a sinner
and was always trying to make up for his sinfulness by being
good. Perhaps he felt that one part goodness would cancel
out one part of sin, the goal always being to stay at least in
the neutral zone or better yet do more good than bad.

Being fearful of God's judgment is a powerful
motivator.   It is one we are not unfamiliar with. After all,
doesn't it say in Philippians to "work out your salvation with
fear and trembling" (Phil. 2:12)? Insecure Christians do
things because they are not sure of themselves, or anyone
else, either. They may hear that once they are saved they
cannot be separated from the love of God and security of the
Savior; but they are not *really* sure this is the case for them.
Mostly, they work overtime just trying to cover up their sins
of the day. So what makes these fearful and insecure
Christians Pharisees? They can't stand others being slack
in their faith. If they are going to work hard for their salvation
and holiness, 'by George' others ought to as well.   Someone
else being secure in their faith is uncomfortable to them, and
someone not working as hard as they do in their faith is
objectionable to them.

Again, John
Fischer in his book, *12
Steps of a Recovering
Pharisee (Like Me)* has
as his 3rd (of 12) step:
[We] "Realize that we
detest mercy being
given to those who,
unlike us, haven't
worked for it and don't
deserve it." [5] Judgementalism comes from an attitude of
contempt. This is easy to do. I know of a guy who is a very
talented speaker and teacher. I have seen him speak and
teach in impromptu sessions in which he had very little if any
preparation. His delivery is dynamic, his grasp of the facts
and material is mind-boggling, and he conveys the message
in a compelling way…so much so that he totally engrosses
the audience. What takes me 15-20 hours or more of study

> Someone else being secure
> in their faith is uncomfortable
> to them, and someone not
> working as hard as they do in
> their faith is objectionable to
> them.

and preparation he can do "off the cuff." After all is done, he does it better and more thoroughly than I and gets more accolades at that. This ticks me off! Don't people know how much I prepare? Don't they realize what I've put into this? How come after all I've done, he still gets all the glory? (Well, there I am, comparing again...part of the Pharisaical Lure)

But fear develops spiritual hypertension. A Fearing Pharisee does his or her thing out of anxiety and being uptight, a kind of hyper-Christian, in need of some spiritual valium, never resting, just like Martha, always trying to stay ahead of the game. They are motivated by nagging questions of "When it's all over, will God really accept them and receive them into the kingdom?" And even today, will they be accepted by other Christians, particularly those in leadership, if they don't do more?

Selling indulgences, and doing penance—climbing up stairs on your knees, or saying 'X' amount of spiritual phrases are motivated out of fear. Every act becomes an act of spiritual penance. So all your good works aren't really good anymore because they are tainted with an ulterior motive...to cancel out badness with enough goodness. And this fear stays with those of us who are dominated with this trait. It is our ever present reminder because we can never quite get there...we can never quite make it...we are never quite good enough. All this leads to spiritual frustration and a sense of incompleteness. A low and unhealthy self-image; a low and meager Christian self-image.

God-Fearing Pharisee

Finally, there was the God-Fearing Pharisee. This was the genuine article, someone who truly loved God and wanted to please Him. I imagine this kind of Pharisee was quite rare, because when you consider the Pharisaical Lure and the syndrome that pulls us into self-righteousness; it's pretty hard to escape. Yet, unencumbered by the other self-righteous legalists, there were some who apparently stayed away from the traps and the lure. Quite frankly, it sounds more like a fantasy and lore than reality. How you could be a "Pharisee," and be associated with that bunch, and somehow stay true to God's Word—the spirit of the Word—and unaffected by the group, to me seems impossible. In fact, a God-Fearing and "godly" Pharisee seems more like an oxymoron than anything else. I just hope we as Christians don't have the same reputation. On the other hand, I could be pharisaical about the Pharisees!

And so there you have it, seven types of Pharisees, which pretty much covers all the bases. If you can't see yourself in any of these you were probably distracted by thinking of how these apply to others in your life. In your mind, you probably have pinpointed which ones apply to which people you know, who by the way, should read this book so that can be corrected.

What about you? I would like to invite you to go back and review, and if you are bold enough ask some of the closer people in your life which type of Pharisee applies more to you. Owning who we are is the first step toward being who we need to be. Accepting that one or several of these types of Pharisees may apply to you is the first step of breaking the Pharisaical Lure.

Chapter 6

Standards and Assumptions…
the "Not Enough Syndrome"
The Pharisaical Lure continued

"So the Pharisees and teachers of the law asked Jesus, 'Why don't your disciples live according to the tradition of the elders…'" Mark 7:5

There is another aspect of the Pharisaical Lure in which there is a connection between setting standards and our presumptions or assumptions of someone else's motives. We judge people not only by their actions (or lack thereof) but make assumptions regarding their motives and judge these too.

Not enough

We may assume that they are not as dedicated, motivated, or passionate about their godliness [as we are] because they "don't _____ enough". Consistent with what we have already talked about in the Pharisaical Lure and the syndrome associated with it, as we begin to live out in real life the things we "work on," we begin to develop our own spiritual habits, and after awhile get pretty good at them.

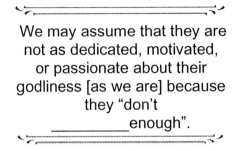

We may assume that they are not as dedicated, motivated, or passionate about their godliness [as we are] because they "don't _____ enough".

Consequently, we look around and see others not doing what we are doing...or at least "not enough."[†]

We assume what their motives are, which is something we can never know unless the person clearly states his or her intentions.

The danger is that we should not assume someone does not love the Lord, or does not desire to please Him because they are not doing something "enough," based upon our standards or spiritual habits. On the back of Mike Yaconelli's book, *Messy Spirituality,* these nagging questions are confronted:

> I guess I'm not a very good Christian...Do you feel like: I don't pray enough; I don't read my Bible enough; I don't share my faith enough; I don't love God enough; I'm not committed enough; I'm not spiritual enough....Then this book is for you. Messy Spirituality was written for the silent majority of us who have been convinced that we just don't do Christianity right.[back of book cover] [1]

More importantly, to judge a person's heart would put us in the same position as the Pharisee and the tax collector (as described earlier). And we know that "The Lord does not look at the things man looks at. Man looks at the outward

---

[†] At this point, if you have been working with a study group on this you will recall that the "not enough" syndrome is included in the *Pharisee Prevention Handbook.* If you would like the handbook you can order it through *Reality Check Resources* at www.realitycheckresources.com

appearance, but the Lord looks at the heart" (1 Samuel 16:7).

Regardless of knowing this we still do it. The "not enough" syndrome is a subtle yet compelling aspect of the Pharisaical Lure. It goes to the issue of comparing we discussed a couple of chapters ago. It is such an important part of the Pharisaical Lure that it is worth talking about in detail here. Simply because we become standard bearers by which we feel others should be gauged. We want everybody to be on the same page and follow the course we are on. We are uncomfortable and uptight when they are not. When they don't "see it" my way, that means either they are wrong or I am wrong...right? And since I am sure I am not wrong, they should do what I do.

The "not enough" syndrome is the nagging nemesis of the Pharisaical Lure. After all, how often have you heard someone say, "he or she doesn't do ____enough". You can fill in the blank. Perhaps you have felt judged or condemned because someone said or implied that you "don't ____enough". My contention with my parents was that they didn't memorize Scripture "enough". Although they knew John 3:16 and a few other verses by heart, I was sure that their spirituality was lagging because they weren't memorizing like I was.

I've been in churches in which evangelism was its key tenant. Nothing is more important than evangelism to them and they continually hammer this thought from the pulpit. The implication, if not outright stated, is that most Christians—and especially those sitting in the seats of this Church—are not evangelizing enough. Most people walk out motivated by guilt rather than excitement. (I will talk more about how this is perpetuated in Chapter 9 in which we will consider *Four Ways Spiritual Leaders Become Pharisees*.)

In other cases I have witnessed pastors and leaders "exhorting" their congregations to give more. If there is a shortfall in the income stream of the congregation they will be given a diet of stories of how such-and-such a person has given not 10% but 15%; or I hear of a congregation challenged to do "reverse tithing" and give 90% of their income, although "only" for a short period of time.

What's being communicated then is that those who don't give a certain amount are not giving enough. I have even heard of congregations where members were told to declare what their income was so that the leaders could monitor the giving, or hold them "accountable" for the tithe that the Lord requires.

Packaged with this, you would get the usual stories of the widow giving her mite, or the family that sacrificed their vacation money for the church building fund. But for the average run-of-the-mill Christian who is barely getting by, all they know is that they are not giving enough while others are. They are lesser Christians than the "givers" within the congregation.

The compulsion seems to be for everyone to follow in line. We mistake uniformity for unity. Obedience is the same measure for everyone; obedience to me should be obedience to you. We disregard our legalism and put it in the category of "discipline". We want conformity to our standards; so you must be "obedient" and "disciplined" in the same way and in the same things as I am. But as Bob George points out, "You will find that a characteristic of legalists is that they always want to "cherry-pick" their favorite laws."[2]

We do this because then, in our minds, things fall into place...that is, a "place" that I can manage. I then can engage in the spiritual "one-upmanship" where I can't point to others who don't do "enough" according to my own standards. John Fischer underlines this reality when he says, "The act of judging gives us a subjective means of affirming ourselves. No matter what I've done or how bad I am, I can always comfort myself by finding someone out there who is "worse" than I am... If I can show that I am better than someone else--anyone else--then I can think of myself as being worthy based on that assessment alone."[3]

What we want is a neat and tidy Christianity; everyone doing the same thing in the same way and in the same amount. What we don't want is what Mike Yaconelli describes in the title of his book, *Messy Spirituality*. He questions our standards and assumptions this way:

> Is there a spirituality for the rest of us who are not secluded in a monastery, who don't have it all together and probably never will?....
>
> Scandalous? Maybe.
>
> Maybe truth is scandalous. Maybe the scandal is that all of us are in some condition of not-togetherness, even those of us who are trying to b e godly. Maybe we're all a mess, not only sinful messy but inconsistent messy, up-and-down messy, in-and-out messy, now-I-believe-now-I-don't messy, I-get-it-now-I-don't-get-it messy, I-understand-uh-now-I-don't-understand messy. I admit, messy spirituality sounds...well...unspiritual.[4]

But we plainly don't like that, because that would mean I would have to give the other guys and gals some slack. Accepting messiness would mean that I can't impose my standards and assumptions on others. It means that I can't manipulate them with the burden of guilt that they are not doing something "enough"; thinking that if I can convince them they are not doing something enough, then they will be motivated to do it enough (like I am). And if I give them too much slack, I lose all control! Plus, it makes me question *my* standards, which I am sure are right because they are Biblical.

Reminding you of my own definition of what a Pharisee is applies here:

> *"I am a Pharisee when I set up precise standards or actions which I have determined equate to righteousness, holiness, and obedience; and judge others in relationship to my own ability to meet those standards [**even when I use Scripture**] ."*

Pharisees don't like broad terms or categories, they want precise standards. They want to know EXACTLY what they are supposed to do, how much they are to do it, so that they can know when they've accomplished whatever it is. It's a type of spiritual competitiveness. Pharisees want to be winners, they want to know that they can out-pace the field; but in order to do that they've got to know how far they've got to go. It's a goal orientation. After all, how will you ever know if you are really spiritual?

In college I knew of a godly couple who had spent forty years in Nigeria as missionaries. I went over to their home several times just to listen to them talk about their life on the mission field, and more importantly to watch how they were living their life in the present. They were older people who didn't seem to have the best of health, but they were the most humble and unpretentious people I had known. They believed that their ministry in their retirement years was a ministry of prayer. In fact, if I recall correctly they had a prayer list of 3,000 plus people, and found myself blessed to be on their list. What they did was divide the list in two, half for each of them, then allot the names out over a period of time. They would have two separate prayer sessions, each individually, one in the morning for a couple of hours and one in the afternoon for a couple of hours, rotating the names until they completed the list weeks or a month later, when they would start all over again trading the lists with each other.

The point of this story is this: never did they imply or insinuate to me that I didn't pray enough. Never did they try to challenge me to do the same or to go by their standard. This was *their* calling and *their* discipline. I always left them feeling blessed, stimulated and encouraged in my walk with the Lord. Yes, as a result, I prayed over my own list. But I never felt like this was a universal standard. I felt encouraged and not guilty simply because they did NOT get sucked into the "not enough syndrome".

The "not enough syndrome" is part of the Pharisaical Lure because it is something that comes naturally to us; therefore, it is something we need to be aware of. If we can own up to the reality of the "not enough" syndrome, we will go a long way to reducing its frequent flare ups and its power over us.

Men Pleasers

The overriding result of the "not enough" syndrome is that it produces men pleasers rather than God pleasers. We first feel guilty for not doing something "enough" and then end up exerting our effort toward that thing that we are not doing enough so that we can fit in, be accepted, and gain the praise of man. The "enough" that we are trying to do is based upon the judgment and standards of man, and the motivation to please men—not God.

> It was the *leading men* who were seeking approval of the leading "spiritual" men, kind of like spiritual politics, spiritual networking and spiritual positioning.

While this is connected with what we will talk about in the chapter on *Blind Guides*, it is more directly tied to the "not enough" syndrome, because it is directly the result of living a guilt ridden life, producing a man-pleasing life. John pointed this out in his gospel:

> And yet [in spite of all this] many even of the leading men (the authorities and nobles) believed and trusted in Him. But

63

because of the Pharisees they did not confess it, for fear that [if they should acknowledge Him] they would be expelled from the synagogue; for they loved the approval and the praise and the glory that come from men [instead of and] more than the glory that comes from God. [They valued their credit with men more than their credit with God.] (John 12:42.43, Amplified Bible)

Loving the approval and praise of man is a strong motivator, then and today. While all of us must confess a tendency toward wanting to please men over God, spiritual hobnobbing is the work of the spiritual elite. As you will note in this text, it was the *leading men* who were seeking approval of the leading "spiritual" men, kind of like spiritual politics, spiritual networking and spiritual positioning. Jockeying for position, the social leaders try to get next to the spiritual leaders hoping to win their favor. How they are perceived and viewed by the spiritual leaders will go a long way to adding favor to their constituency, and to the masses. They become more "spiritual" by association.

Sometimes elder boards and consistories are the direct result of this phenomenon. The more popular, outgoing, and "connected" leaders in the community are the ones who find themselves on the elder board. Then there are those who are perceived as the most spiritual, because they've accumulated spiritual points by being at the church every time the doors are open, or leading prayer in just the right way, or being knowledgeable, or any number of things which get them noticed by those with influence. It's the visibility that's important. Such is the case when we are motivated by a desire to please men, or a misunderstanding of what it means to please God.

Even as I write this, I am painfully aware of the situation in our culture that requires that I seek credibility by association. As we produced my video series of the same name, before this book was written, and as my agent was promoting my work and me to publishers, distributors, and churches, the most common question was, "Who is John Elzinga?" To gain that credibility I need to get two or three (although more is better) popular or identifiable "names" to endorse my work or to write a word or two about how this work may be beneficial to you. Virtually every book you buy, on the back, has three to five testimonials from famous personalities who have read the book and endorse it. Unfortunately, the work can't stand on its own; it needs to be endorsed by someone more popular in order to be read! Although, those with influence don't know me either, so I can't get their endorsement. Credibility is accounted to us by those we associate with. If you can't get connected to the "big guys," you're nobody. Such was the case of the nobles and leaders of the day. They got more accolades by associating with the Pharisees than with Jesus.

This situation is not easily explained as their fault but is our fault; and the fault of a sinful human nature that clamors for attention and self-interest. Eating of the "tree of knowledge of good and evil" was a sin of self-interest, and self-aggrandizement. Every time we buy into the "not enough" syndrome, and as a result pursue something, some new spiritual habit, in order to do it "enough," we need to question if we are doing it to please men or God. We need to consider if we are doing it to gain the accolades of man.

Being A Pharisee While Pursuing Holiness and Obedience

Possibly one of the more puzzling statements Jesus makes is this, "...unless your righteousness surpasses [some versions say "exceed"] that of the Pharisees and the teachers of the law, you will certainly not enter the kingdom of heaven" (Matthew 5; 17-20, esp. vs. 20, NIV).

What? After all we've been talking about regarding the draw and pull of self-righteousness, now Jesus is telling us to be better than the Pharisees? To make matters worse, when we back up a little we read, "...not the smallest letter, not the least stroke of a pen, will by any means disappear from the Law until everything is accomplished" (vs. 18).

This is the famous "jot and tittle" Scripture. The jot was the smallest letter in the Hebrew alphabet. It was similar to an apostrophe ('); while the "tittle" –the least stroke—was similar to one side of the foot of our capital letter (I) (as described in William Barclay's Commentary, *The Daily Study Bible*)

Our contention all along is that we become Pharisaical while pursuing holiness and obedience. Now, we read that Jesus tells us that our righteousness must *exceed* that of the Pharisees? What is this all about? Do you mean to say that we are supposed to be better, more holy, and more obedient than the Pharisees? How does that square with what we have been talking about?

This comes to the core of our issue. We have seen how the Pharisaical Lure and the cycle or syndrome associated with it draws us unwittingly and usually unknowingly into self-righteousness and legalism. We have seen that our own pursuits of obedience and holiness turn into the establishment of standards which we set and tend to use as measures of other's spirituality; ultimately charging others with a claim that they don't "do _____enough." Now when we begin to get the picture we are face to face with a reality that is almost incomprehensible and daunting. It is a challenge I simply can't handle.

Jesus says that not one part of the law will pass away (until he comes again), and then, concerning that law, we are to better at obeying it than the Pharisees. This is a load that is unbearable and leaves me feeling helpless and hopeless. Jesus hammers the Pharisees and their distortion of the law, their self-righteousness, legalism, and judgementalism, and now he tells me to be better than them?! Confusing? Frustrating? Yes!

I believe that he was and is trying to get our attention. This statement should jar us. First, if we look at the immediate context of Matthew 5:21-48, and then if we look at the overall context from Matthew chapter 5 through chapter 7 we see Jesus turning everything around. He was setting the record straight, he was pointing out a new way of understanding, not that it was new; rather, it is like the designer telling us his original intention of the law and ultimately how we should live our lives. He is giving us a new paradigm, a new way of seeing. Once again, not that it is new, but it allows us to see it from a different light. Now that He is here, now that the Messiah is present, now that his kingdom has come (and will come to completion with his next coming) we should see things as they really are.

Immediately after he talks about our righteousness surpassing that of the Pharisees he reveals a staggering thought—to the disciples, to the crowd, and to the Pharisees that were listening in—IT DOESN'T TAKE THE ACT TO COMMIT SIN, ALL IT TAKES IS THE THOUGHT; and because of this reality, everyone is in the same boat!

He goes on to describe *how* everyone is in the same boat: to be considered a murderer all you have to do is be angry, to commit adultery all you have to do is lust, basically any divorce creates a situation for adultery, now any oath you take is binding, an eye for an eye now becomes turn the other cheek, and love your neighbor becomes love your enemies. He goes on in chapter 6: give to the needy without anyone knowing; do not pray in public where you can be seen but behind closed doors; don't tell people you are fasting and don't look like it either; and so on. WOW! Looking at is this way, there's no way that I *can't* sin! I'm trapped, stuck, destined to fail...how in the world is my righteousness supposed to EXCEED that of the Pharisees if all I have to do to sin is lust or get angry, or not fulfill all of my promises or intentions, or not love my enemy?

Before answering this dilemma, I believe Jesus leads us to a key point that must be viewed within this context:

> Do not judge, or you too will be judged. For in the same way you judge others, you will be judged, and with the measure you use, it will be measured to you. Why do you look at the speck of sawdust in your brother's

eye and pay no attention to the plank in your own eye? How can you say to your brother, 'Let me take the speck out of your eye,' when all the time there is a plank in your own eye? You hypocrite, first take the plank out of your eye, and then you will see clearly to remove the speck from your brother's eye (Matthew 7:1-5).

For those who are concerned about church discipline and "accountability" the tendency here would be to focus on the part of this Scripture that says once you remove your plank, then you can see clearly to remove the speck from your brother. In other words, they would say, "It doesn't say, 'don't judge or hold accountable', all it says it that I first must remove my log". The implication here is that we first must get our act together *before* we can judge someone else. But we want to twist this just a little and imply that we actually can get our act together and get the log out (of our eye), thus freeing us up to judge.

To these people I have a few questions: based upon what Jesus said, we are ALL major sinners (we all lust, therefore committing adultery; we all get angry with others therefore making us murderers; we all violate oaths and promises; we all have a tendency to hate our enemy; etc), so how can we ever get the log out? Are we ever so righteous, clean and pure that we never have a right to even talk about the speck in our brother's eye? While I don't have a definitive answer, nor do I want to be guilty of judging the judger, I do believe that we are to struggle with these issues. The issues of "accountability" are more foggy than clear; and I think that is exactly what Jesus is cautioning here.

To unravel this dilemma let me leave you with a couple of concepts which can shed light on this dilemma and help us to live our lives more freely.

First, we have misinterpreted the goal of the Christian life. Dallas Willard in his profound book, *The Divine Conspiracy*, talks about the "gospel of sin management." We have been misled into believing that the key to the

Christian life is to get out of sin—getting saved and our sin removed. Once we have that taken care of, we can move on and do what we want; implying here that once we are saved nothing else matters. He says,

> History has brought us to the point where the Christian message is thought to be essentially concerned only with how to deal with sin: with wrongdoing or wrong-being and its effects. Life, our actual existence, is not included in what is now presented as the heart of the Christian message, or it is included only marginally.....The current gospel then becomes a "gospel of sin management." Transformation of life and character is no part of the redemptive message. Moment-to-moment human reality in its depths is not the arena of faith and eternal living.[5]

My own pastor, Dr. Stephen Stuikmans, says in his Bible study on the book of Romans, that "we are not sinners because we commit sins; no—we sin because we are sinners by birth. The fact that we sin is merely the evidence that we already are sinners!" He continues later, "As shocking as it may sound, the goal of the Christian life is not to stop sinning! No, the real goal of the normal Christian life is to know Christ and to allow Him to live His life in you and through you." The point here is that we misunderstand thinking that the goal of the Christian life is NOT to sin, because we cannot not sin. We are sinners. We have a sin problem. It is a double problem because we are sinners positionally. That is who we are, we are born with a sin nature; and we sin...day by day, moment by moment. How, then can we exceed the righteousness of the Pharisees?

The other clue that Jesus gives is toward the beginning when he lays out these concepts. In Matthew 5:17 he says, "Do not think that I have come to abolish the law and the prophets; I have not come to abolish them but to *fulfill* them." (NIV) [emphasis mine] The key question is, what does he mean by "fulfill"?

Fulfill here means to complete, to make whole. He is the missing link that completes the chain, and makes the chain strong and usable. He is the fulfiller. With Christ inserted into the scenario of bumbling attempts to be obedient, holy and righteous we see that we can't do it without Him. He does what we could never do.

I think that the point Jesus is making is that our righteousness is placed in Him, that our ability to keep the law

> It is only through Him that we can live with the freedom to do things without running around worrying about our sin, much less the sin of our brother and sister.

is impossible, but He fulfills it, completes it, and we are to place our confidence in Him. Only he can do what we can never do; only he can fulfill what we can never fulfill. It is only through Him that we can live with the freedom to do things without running around worrying about our sin, much less the sin of our brother and sister.

Augustine said, "Love the Lord and live how you want." The key question is not "Are you a Christian?" The key question in life is "Do you love the Lord?" What's the difference? Dallas Willard's concept of the gospel of sin management puts things in their proper perspective. The issue in life is not getting "in" in order to get rid of sin; then to move on. The issue in life is not running around like Pharisees trying to manage our sin. John Fischer would call this, "...the practice of engineering sins to a size one can control while missing all the huge implications of the deeds, thoughts, and intents of the heart." [6]

The issue in life is loving the Lord! If you love the Lord all other issues fall into place. Because if you love the Lord, you will live for the Lord. Your goal in life is to live to please Him. My goal in life is not to run around correcting my brother, because I have a plank in my eye. I don't see

70

clearly looking at others, but my focus should be on the Lord and what he has done for me—my own sin.

There is a story I've read about a good man dying and going to heaven. I modify it here a little for the purposes of this piece. We will call this man a modern day Pharisee. The story goes: There was a modern day Pharisee who, after a long and good life, died and went to heaven. At the gates of heaven he met Saint Peter who said that he needed 100 points to get in. For every good thing he did in life, Peter would award him some points, and when he accumulated 100 he could get in. Well, this modern day Pharisee thought to himself, "That's all? This is going to be easy!" So he said to Saint Peter, "Okay, well I've been married to the same woman for 50 years and never once was unfaithful, not even in my mind." Peter, said, "That's good, for that I will give you 2 points". "Two points…that's all?" the modern day Pharisee thought to himself. So he said, "Okay, I've got another one: I was an elder in my church, whenever the church doors were open I was there, and I tithed 10% of my gross income." Peter said, "That's great, for that I will give you 1 point." The modern day Pharisee couldn't believe his ears! Just one point for all that? So he said, to Peter, "alright, this one should do it, I gave to the poor and served at the community soup kitchen and homeless shelter every holiday season." Peter said, "Wonderful! For that I will give you 2 more points." "Only two points? I can't believe this," and so in frustration, this modern day Pharisee…this tremendously good man said, "At this rate I'll only get in by the grace of God!" Peter said, "Precisely!" "You now have 100 points, go on in!"[7]

Ultimately, our life isn't about our goodness (as my Pastor keeps reminding us), nor is it about our management of sin. It is about God's grace, both in the act of salvation and in the life we now live.

But Jesus just didn't leave it here; he gave us warning signs and indicators of when we have crossed "over the line" and into the arena of pharisaicalism. It is to these warning signs we now turn.

71

Chapter 7

Warning Signs and Dangers of the Pharisaical Lure

"Woe to you...you hypocrites..."
Matt. 23:13, 15, 16, 23, 25, 27, 29

Jesus recognized that the Pharisee's problem was not in their blatant and bold sinfulness, but rather in their subtle and manipulative methods and tactics; in their tendencies and traits. These "seven woes" as they are referred to, are significant because seven times Jesus says, "Woe to you...you hypocrites..." as he chastises the Pharisees for their deceptiveness, trying to bring them out of their state of denial.

You see, self-righteousness has a way of being accepted, duplicated, and honored; it does so precisely because it seems so righteous, pure, and holy. How can you criticize someone for being "obedient"? How can you chastise someone for being, well, so...spiritual? And so pharisaicalism has a built-in reinforcement program.

The problem is that we don't recognize it for what it is—self-righteousness and legalism. We want to call it something else. We want to call it discipline; we want to refer to what we do as godly habits; we want to refer to it as becoming more mature. All the while we are creating a self-supporting system of pharisaical divisiveness. And here's the key: we don't do this intentionally!

You see, self-righteousness has a way of being accepted, duplicated, and honored; it does so precisely because it seems so righteous, pure, and holy.

As we go through these seven woes I would like to challenge you to resist the temptation to think or say, "Well, that was the Pharisees, they were a problem! Or to say it another way, don't be Pharisaical about the Pharisees, and self-righteously say to yourself, "Thank God I am not like those Pharisees." This is stuff WE DO, and things we must wrestle with. Acknowledge it, own it, and move on!

I have taken each woe and tried to identify them with something analogous to today's world. If you have the study guide you will be encouraged to enter into a discussion about each woe. Try to come up with your own thoughts regarding how we violate these woes today. The thoughts I offer here are not definitive or the end of the matter; you or your group may come up with other conceptions of how these woes play a part in our evangelical world.

Woe Number 1: The Kingdom Repellers (Matthew 23:13)

"Woe to you, teachers of the law and Pharisees, you hypocrites! You shut the kingdom of heaven in men's faces. You yourselves do not enter, nor will you let those enter who are trying to."

This woe is about the concept of attracting new believers into the kingdom. It is about what the seeker is seeing within our community of faith. When they come into our churches and investigate or get a little closer to coming to faith—what is it that they see? Do they see a caring community of Christ followers or do they see a system of Christian living and holiness that is more cumbersome than it is caring? Is it a compelling, living message of God's grace or is it a system of rules and regulations that is more repelling than it is compelling?

This is what Jesus was talking about here. He was telling the Pharisees with all their rules and regulations, with their system of legalism and their myriad of steps on how to be obedient, that they were making it impossible for anyone to enter into the kingdom, and Jesus points out, based upon the system they've set up, that they will not be entering either.

I will be talking about this a little further in the chapter on *Leaders as Pharisees*, but for now the point is that we as a Christian community are often perceived as stuffy, legalistic, boring, and not relevant to the very people we are trying to attract. Bill Hybels communicates this in his book and concept of *Contagious Christianity*. The essence of the life that we live should be contagious and irresistible. Instead, we often portray a belief system that is almost claustrophobic, creating an atmosphere that closes in on people making them feel like they can't breath. We need to give people breathing room.

When I grew up, the concept of not working on Sunday was prevalent within the church we attended. My parents, trying to be obedient, wouldn't let me play on Sunday. I can't tell you how many Sundays I spent looking out my bedroom window watching my neighbor friends play basketball in my neighbor's driveway. Later, they relaxed these rules a little: If I stayed in my yard, I could play catch— I just couldn't play ball. I could shoot hoops—I just couldn't play a game of basketball. I could throw the football—I just couldn't play in a neighborhood scrimmage. Since most of my friends were non-Christians, I always wondered what they thought, and I never really knew how to explain this to them, mostly because I didn't understand it myself; it seemed so confusing and unappealing. In many ways I lived a double life, one that conformed to the systems set up by my parent's interpretation of our church's beliefs and the other hanging with my friends with very little connection of one to the other. My life within the church seemed to be defined by what I couldn't do, rather than what I could do. Concerning my non-Christian friends I always wondered, if this is what Christianity is all about, then why would they be interested in a religion like this?

Now don't get me wrong here, I'm not talking about losing your grip on sound theology. Good doctrine and sound theology are very important. I am more likely to draw lines and fences with theological issues than with life issues. There are bad, even heretical theologies floating around out there. There are teachings floating around that equate to what Paul talks about when he says they worship "a different Jesus" (than the one he was preaching about). But we often mistake our church systems...the way we look, act, and the rules we set up, for theology. It is not the same.

> Examine your system and see if it is something that pushes people away rather than something that brings them into the kingdom.

When someone comes into your church are they greeted or ignored? Are the clothes they are wearing an issue in your church...will they feel that they "fit in" or feel ostracized? Is the worship compelling to them, inviting to them? Is the message something they will get or at least sometime that will make them think, or is it something filled with code words that no one understands? Again, don't get me wrong, I'm not talking about watering down our faith and creating what I call "Diet Christianity" or what some refer to as "Christian Light". (If you would like more information on this, I have two messages that talk about each of these subjects; the first is Go for the Ah Ha...rather than wait for the Uh Oh—a message about change within the church; the second is Super-Spiritual Christianity which talks about our lack of serious study and teaching within the evangelical community.)

Examine your system and see if it is something that pushes people away rather than something that brings them into the kingdom. I encourage you to struggle with this question: what makes a contagious person contagious in the first place? This is a question I believe every church fellowship needs to wrestle with.

Woe #2: Blindly Devoted Followers (Matthew 23:15)

"Woe to you, teachers of the law and Pharisees, you hypocrites! You travel over land and sea to win a single convert, and when he becomes one, you make him twice as much a son of hell as you are."

As with the Pharisees, sometimes we focus so strongly on a person's conversion, that once they are converted they become more Pharisaical than the Pharisees. In other words, some people are blindly devoted followers. They convert because they've caved into the pressure, or they are attracted to the charisma of a person or succumbing to a group to which they are attached. And when they follow, they follow hook, line, and sinker! They are now fierce and unrelenting followers of a person or a particular church, rather than drawn into a real relationship with a living Savior.

Cult-like conditions are sometimes created within our church fellowships. What is indicative of a cult? What are the ingredients that make a cult a cult? What's the difference between a cult and a healthy, living, breathing congregation faithfully following the risen Lord?

Merriam-Webster dictionary defines a cult as *"great devotion to a person, idea, object, movement, or work (as a film or book)...a usually small group of people characterized by such devotion."* But the mistake is to be made if we think that cult joining is done with eyes wide open. Most who join cults don't think of themselves as joining a cult. Our focus here is the "blind" part of being a devoted follower.

Jacques Ellul, the French-Christian sociologist, has studied the how leaders and groups influence those within their grasp and has identified it with the concept of propaganda in a book of the same name. He says,

> Sociological propaganda is a phenomenon much more difficult to grasp than political propaganda, and is rarely discussed. Basically it is the penetration of an ideology by means of its sociological context... Instead it is based on a general climate, an atmosphere that influences people imperceptibly without having the appearance of propaganda; it gets to man through his customs, through his most unconscious habits. It creates new habits in him; it is a sort of persuasion from within.[1]

If you can forget about the word propaganda for a moment and consider what he has identified as a dynamic of the follower (whether individually or groups, organizations, and yes, churches) you will see how *followership* can be blind, or at least farsighted—not seeing things clearly that are close to us. It's scary how volatile we as humans are; even we Christians.

The point of this woe is that the Pharisaical control over people first comes from the leader and the system. That is, there is a dynamic coming from the leadership, whether it be a single person, or a group of leaders in which they captivate the attention of the listener or observer. It borders on hypnosis, mind control, or brainwashing. We could even refer to it as "heart control."

This is the case of Pharisees producing other Pharisees. Those that have joined the group—or we could say the Pharisaical congregation—have become spellbound by the life and message of the group they are joining. Or they are so captivated by the charismatic teaching of the main guy (in our case, Pastors/Preachers/Teachers) that they suck up everything they say like a sponge. Ellul points out: "There is no equality; the members accept leadership, and of course small groups also recognize instituted authorities. Dominant personalities play a considerable role, and often group opinion will be formed by individuals who are known to all the members of the group, and whose authority is accepted." [2]

We will talk about this extensively in the chapter on *Blind Guides*, but for now let us agree about a couple things:

1. Pharisees try to produce more Pharisees or at least attract wannabe Pharisees.
2. Those that are brought into the group become fanatical and uncritical proponents of the group, church, or pastor.

Jesus here is saying, "woe to you who have this kind of hold on people" and, "Woe to you who follow and become like these leaders." No one escapes this woe, not even the followers. The key here is the aspect of uncritically following someone or some group. I know of a church which set up a system of church discipline in which "insubordination" is one of their proponents and a "reason" for disciplining someone within the church. This is both unbiblical and is the very reason cults are created. To question, challenge, or disagree with the leadership who have been considered "ordained" by God is considered a rebellious or a contentious spirit...or insubordination.

Funny thing, though: the Bereans apparently questioned and researched what Paul said and what he taught. In Acts17:11 it says that they "...examined the Scriptures every day to see if what Paul say was true." Apparently, they had questions, doubts, and even challenged what Paul was saying.

And for that Paul said, "You are guilty of insubordination and need to submit yourself to my teaching??" No, rather, commenting on their response, Scripture says, "Now the Bereans were of *more noble character* than the Thessalonians." [emphasis mine] Because they were willing to think critically they were considered "more noble" than the

Thessalonians. Yet, today, for fear of being critical we no longer engage in critical thinking. Questioning, challenging, debating, and even disagreement are not signs of insubordination or rebellion but are important in the process of insuring that the truth is being preached and taught consistent with Scripture. As with the Bereans, this should be encouraged and praised; it should be something we are always engaged in.

The message here to the pastor-teacher is that if you are casting your spell upon people, perhaps threatening and manipulating them with the fear of church discipline because they are disagreeing with you, perhaps you yourself are guilty of being Pharisaical. If you are a follower, uncritically taking in all that is presented to you without checking it out for yourself, and if you have become an uncritical follower of such a person, group, or church; watch out, you may be a victim of the Pharisaical Lure and are perpetuating to others you know that the teaching of your leader or group is the only way to be a real Christian.

But again, we must recognize the "blindly" aspect of devoted followers. Most people, including most Christians, think of themselves as fairly adept at being able to discern truth from falsehood, and few feel any sense of danger. One final warning comes from Jacques Ellul's writings:

> Naturally, the educated man does not believe in propaganda; he shrugs and is convinced that propaganda has no effect on him. This is, in fact, one of his great weaknesses, and propagandists are well aware that in order to reach someone, one must first convince him that propaganda is ineffectual and not very clever. Because he is convinced of his own superiority, the intellectual is much more vulnerable than anybody else to their maneuver...[3]

The encouragement here is to check things out for yourself, and to be discerning enough to question and challenge what is being taught, no matter who is teaching it. If we didn't have the likes of Luther, Calvin, Farrell, Zwingli and many of the Reformers we would have never broken free from the controlling spell the Catholic church had on its members back in the days of the Reformation.

Certainly not as dramatically, if we didn't have the likes of Bill Hybels or others in the 70's challenging the way we "do church" we would never have had the opportunity to reach so many who would otherwise not walk through the doors of a traditional church. Testing and questioning the boundaries is part of our responsibility and will dismantle the power of the Pharisaical Lure.

Woe #3: Looking for Loop Holes (Matthew 23:16-22)

"Woe to you, blind guides! You say, 'If anyone swears by the temple, it means nothing; but if anyone swears by the gold of the temple, he is bound by his oath.' You blind fools! Which is greater: the gold, or the temple that makes the gold sacred? You also say, 'If anyone swears by the altar, it means nothing; but if anyone swears by the gift on it, he is bound by his oath.' You blind men! Which is greater: the gift, or the altar that makes the gift sacred? Therefore, he who swears by the altar swears by it and by everything on it. And he who swears by the temple swears by it and by the one who dwells in it. And he who swears by heaven swears by God's throne and by the one who sits on it."

As I've said before, the Pharisees were spiritual technicians. They were into being very precise and exact. They were into detail. They wanted to get it right, and wanted everyone else to get it right as well. The letter of the law was what it was all about. This gave them two distinct "powers" over people, spiritually speaking. The first was that they could always point out how people were not keeping the law, how they fell short. Secondly, they developed "loopholes" with which they could get away with things that weren't convenient for them.

As William Barclay explains in *The Daily Study Bible* commentary, this is a case in which the Pharisees believed that some oaths were binding while others were not. He explains,

> To the Jew an oath was absolutely binding, so long as it was a binding oath. Broadly speaking, a binding oath was an oath which definitely and without equivocation employed the name of God; such an oath must be kept, no matter what the cost. Any other oath might be legitimately broken. The idea was that, if God's name was actually used, then God was introduced as a partner into the transaction, and to break the oath was not only to break faith with men but to insult God.[4]

Jesus was basically saying, "Listen, whatever oath you take is binding. Don't try to weasel out of something because you have determined it's not binding." The loophole concept is really a matter of a lack of integrity. Today, we cross our fingers, or appeal to the technicality: "I didn't say that, what I said was....." "That's what you heard, but not what I said." "That was then, but this is now." "Yeah, I said I would do it—I just didn't say when."

If we are sharp, we may intentionally design a loop hole or two into our commitments by leaving out some essential thing so that when we are challenged to keep our commitments we can point out that "technically speaking" this is what it meant. Therefore, we have built in a point of "flexibility" into our commitment. People make commitments, they're just not committed. People often commit to something only to renege on that commitment if something better comes along and then they will commit to that. Appealing to technicalities is a favorite tactic of the Pharisee.

Jesus said in Matthew 5:37, "Simply let your 'Yes' be 'Yes', and let your 'No' be 'No'..." Do what you say you will do. Make sure your commitments are clear. Keep to the spirit of the commitment and don't add loopholes that will give you a way out.

Woe #4: Pettiness (Matthew 23:23, 24)

"Woe to you, teachers of the law and Pharisees, you hypocrites! You give a tenth of your spices—mint, dill and cummin. But you have neglected the more important matters of the law—justice, mercy and faithfulness. You should have practiced the latter, without neglecting the former. You blind guides! You strain out a gnat but swallow a camel."

The issue of pettiness falls along the same lines as the loophole issue. It is consistent with the fact that Pharisees were and are spiritual technicians. They have an overwhelming need to be precise and exact...and to make sure everyone keeps to the letter of the law.

In this instance Jesus was using the example of tithing and how ridiculous it was to demand the tithing of "mint, dill, and cumin." The Pharisees of Jesus' day were insistent about tithing on everything. The point of the mint, dill, and cumin takes two things to the extreme: First, and the most obvious, is how miniscule mint, dill, and cumin are. All you have to do is go to your kitchen cupboard and most people will have dill as one of their spices they use to ad flavor to certain foods. Go take a look at it...take out one or two dill seeds. To take the demonstration even further, count out 100 seeds. Now separate 10 seeds from the 100. Can you imagine being concerned about tithing that?

The second issue is pointed out by William Barclay in *The Daily Study Bible*. Jesus was not talking to the farmer here, who was to tithe a portion of his crops (since his crops represented money). Apparently most everyone at that time had their own little herb garden in which they could pick spices for their daily meals. This garden could be only a few plants. In this case, odds are that a person would only need or have one dill plant. The Pharisees, being the spiritual technicians that they were, felt that you had to tithe even from your herb garden, and even from each plant!

This is not only a sensitive subject but it is also a Pharisaical issue within the church. The legalists now will want to swoop in and save you from what I am about to say, and the line drawers are getting their pencils ready. I imagine certain pastors may be worried that if you get this point, they will have to worry about the church budget or the building fund. But tithing has very much been a legalistic issue within some churches.

If tithing is demanded, required, surveyed and recorded within any church I want to suggest to you that they may have crossed the line from a desire to be obedient to God, to outright legalism. Legalism IS pharisaicalism. How do you know where that line is? I invite you to wrestle with where the line is. If you have the DVD and study guide and are studying this as a home group, adult Sunday school class, or even as a church, this is one of the questions you should chew on for awhile.

Let me suggest a few thoughts here. Paul says, "Each man should give what he has decided in his heart, not reluctantly or under compulsion, for God loves a cheerful giver" (2 Corinthians 9:7). I've heard that the correct interpretation of "cheerful" is actually "hilarious". Well, let me tell you that if I'm demanded to give, manipulated to give, or told to give a certain amount in order to be obedient to God, there is nothing hilarious about that. If I am told to announce or declare publicly how much I make and how much I'm going to give, there is nothing cheerful about that. In fact, all this does is create feelings of reluctance and compulsion.

The issue here that Jesus was referring to is that when we get petty, when we focus in on exactness, preciseness, and detail, we begin to major on the minors and make mountains out of molehills. When we do this, we lose the spirit of the issue or concept, and we soon begin to take the heart right out of it. Pettiness has a way of sapping all of the meaning out of an issue and the heart out of the person.

Jesus was saying, "You guys just don't get the point" (about tithing)! And God through Paul had to remind us

AGAIN, in his comment to the Corinthian Church that it's not about how much, it's not about the detail, it's not about the method, and it's not about demand or coercion. It's about what is on your heart to give, that *this* should be a commitment you make TO GOD, and that this should be done in cheerfulness and joy.

I do want to make a side bar note that is pertinent here: as discussed in the loophole issue in the previous section; this is NOT a loophole not to give; nor is it a loophole that says you give a little here and a little there...whatever you feel like at any given moment. There is a commitment involved in giving "as you have purposed in your heart..." And as stressed before, out of integrity we need to keep to our commitments. All oaths are binding oaths.

Now, this is obviously not the forum to discuss in detail all the Biblical and theological aspects of tithing. I will leave you to struggle with this within the confines of your own church fellowship and under the guidance of your Pastor. The point is that if it gets petty, it is legalistic and Pharisaical.

Pettiness doesn't just surround the issue

The issue here that Jesus was referring to is that when we get petty, when we focus in on exactness, preciseness, and detail, we begin to major on the minors and make mountains out of molehills.

of tithing. It is a very Pharisaical tactic and surrounds many issues we focus on. Whenever we take a thing—even a good thing—and take it to the extreme we have a tendency to become petty. In fact, most of the laws, or rather the definitions of the laws that came through the oral tradition, set down by the scribes and practiced by the Pharisees were petty. In their quest to apply it to their lives, they took the law to the absurd. This is the nature of the Pharisaical Lure and the syndrome or cycle associated with it. You can take almost every major issue, from evangelism to prayer, worship to preaching, the gifts of the spirit to spiritual gifts, Scripture memory to biblical study and define it down to every action and sub-action, taking it to the absurd and making it into a petty law…like mint, dill, and cumin.

Woe #5 Mr. Clean (Matthew 23: 25, 26)

"Woe to you, teachers of the law and Pharisees, you hypocrites! You clean the outside of the cup and dish, but inside they are full of greed and self-indulgence. Blind Pharisee! First clean the inside of the cup and dish, and then the outside also will be clean."

The issue here for the Pharisees was about being presentable. It wasn't about being dirty, but rather appearing clean. It wasn't just about looking nice, but looking pure, holy, and obedient. In short, they wanted to look spiritually acceptable, or even more so, spiritually admirable. This is where the whole concept of hypocrisy comes in. To be a hypocrite is literally to be an actor or to play the part. They wanted to look like spiritual giants, so they played the part.

This is where we come in. Washing the "outside of the cup" is something we are good at. The more we work on our image, the more we will be accepted within the evangelical community. Pick up the right lingo, use the right phrases, wear compatible clothes, tell the right stories, read the right books, and we will fit in fine. If we get really good at it, we learn how to act like a mature godly person. The ultimate goal: to be in position for leadership. Not only accepted, but admired.

Some of this is Sociology 101. We all tend to act, walk, dress, talk like those we hang around with. I have spent a fair amount of time traveling for business. I would occasionally make my rounds to Texas…to Dallas, Houston, etc. I don't know what it is about a Texas accent, but it would take me less than a day to start talking with a Texas drawl, or using common buzz words like "fixin to." This is normal stuff, and we all tend to be like those we hang around with.

But what we are talking about here is something more profuse than that. The Pharisees were expert adaptors. Like chameleons, they could portray just the right image of a super-spiritual leader...holy, righteous, and obedient. Of course, they perfected the art of obedience by "living out" the law to the finest detail, as we have pointed out over and over.

> It seems like the better my prayers sound, the more spiritual I am.

For those of us who are guilty of this aspect of pharisaicalism, we don't just want to fit in, we want to look good, or rather, be looked up to. For years growing up, I recall that those who were leaders of the church were pretty good at the way that they prayed. They could pray out loud in public and in groups. They could pray for a long time—some of their prayers were like mini-sermons, and there was something about the way they sounded in their prayer...so majestic, so authoritarian, and so eloquent. So I figured out that if I could learn to sound that way when I prayed that I might become what was perceived as a mature godly person. Although today I don't usually pray that way, I still see some vestiges of it in some of my prayers. Am I the only one inflicted with this problem? It seems like the better my prayers sound, the more spiritual I am.

Unfortunately, if some who have heard my prayers think I'm a spiritual giant they couldn't be further from the truth. I, like Mike Yaconelli, am a messy Christian, I am definitely not above reproach, I have failed more than I have succeeded, I struggle with issues, relationships, and my own sinfulness. But, I can only put on a good image for so long. While I may be able to put on a presentable image in groups, most people that really know me know my weaknesses.

Now here's the dilemma—and if you have the study guide and the video and are working this through with a group I hope you spend some time struggling with this issue—while we all need to grow and mature into "godly" Christians we need to be brutally aware of the temptation to "act" the part rather than just "be" who we are in Christ. I say this because I think the mistake is to think that to be "acting" we need to be consciously aware that this is what we are doing. In other words, the mistake is to think that I am intentionally acting. I think the problem is more subtle than that. I think that we are "taught" how to act a certain way, and those that are modeling a certain way of being are presenting to those that follow that if you want to be a mature, godly person, this is how you will act.

Let me approach this from a slightly different angle. Years ago, when I was involved with the Navigators (not professionally mind you---just as a follower) I could tell the difference between someone who was a "Navigator" and someone who was with Campus Crusade for Christ. They talked about the same things differently, and if you knew what those things were, you could tell the difference. Similarly, I could always tell a Baptist from a Reformed person—by the way they talked, and somewhat by the way they dressed. Today, you can tell if a person is influenced by those in the "word of faith" movement...all you have to do is listen to how they respond to you when you talk. For example, phrases like: "I can't receive that" are indicative of this movement.

Hopefully, you get the picture. The problem revolves around the difference between "being" and "doing."

> Do we really know what a mature godly person looks like? Do we have to act a certain way, look a certain way, and say certain things?

Acting happens when we try to "do" something that will cause us to look like someone we "should" be like. Being is simply allowing the Holy Spirit to work within your life, and be who you are in Christ rather than trying to "be like" someone else or some image that has been presented to you. Dallas Willard makes the following comment concerning the

Beatitudes, which I believe describes the misunderstanding of "doing" (laws) verses "being" (something that comes from the heart):

> The most common "whim," historically, has been the disastrous idea just mentioned: that Jesus is here giving laws. For if that is all he is doing, they will certainly be laws that are impossible to keep... [and he comments previous to this]...he was in fact teaching precisely the futility of any such actions. They would make no difference, because true rightness remains a matter of one's heart. [5]

This leads to the question; do we really know what a mature godly person looks like? Do we have to act a certain way, look a certain way, and say certain things? Is anyone really above reproach as described in passages such as, "Now the overseer must be above reproach..." as found in 1 Timothy 3:2? I ask this because I'm not really sure I know anyone who *really is* above reproach. I think we will go a long way to dismantle the trap of the Pharisaical Lure when we lay down the "false images" of which pure, holy, godly, and obedient people look like, and allow ourselves to just "be" in Christ.

Woe #6: Proud Humility (Matthew 23:27, 28)

> *"Woe to you, teachers of the law and Pharisees, you hypocrites! You are like whitewashed tombs, which look beautiful on the outside but on the inside are full of dead men's bones and everything unclean. In the same way, on the outside you appear to people as righteous but on the inside you are full of hypocrisy and wickedness."*

According to William Barclay's *The Daily Study Bible*, since graveyards were sometimes along-side of pathways and walkways, and since It was considered unclean to even touch a grave, (because dead men's bones lay underneath), it was common practice to whitewash the tomb or grave site, (monument of some kind) so that those walking by the way would know the grave was there and avoid walking on it or accidentally touching it. Similar to washing the outside of the cup, Jesus was commenting on how the Pharisees liked to appear on the outside—clean, holy, righteous, and humble—but underneath their appearance there was deadness. This is why he said, "You are like white-washed tombs..." (vs. 27).

Packaging is everything...at least from a marketing perspective. Even with this book you are reading, and the DVD and study guide; we spent some time and had a couple of options regarding how we wanted the cover graphics to look. We wanted the cover to be striking, interesting, and appealing. We wanted the title to grab you, maybe even have a touch of "controversy" with it, something that goes against the normal grain. We did this so that you would actually pick it up and read it, because inside there might be something that enthralls you.

The Pharisees knew that packaging was everything, and as we discussed earlier, one of the ways the Pharisees liked to package their spirituality was with the appearance of humility. There are few things more attractive, spiritually speaking, than someone who is humble. The older retired couple who were retired missionaries that I mentioned before, were humble; my grandfather was truly humble; I would say that my pastor is humble (and very selfless); but other than that, I have known few genuinely humble people.

We are certainly told in Scripture to be humble; and as with other things associated with the Pharisaical Lure, in the pursuit of humility, although a godly thing; all too often ends up being a self-righteous thing.

A self-righteous humility is a proud humility. The bearer of this kind of "humility" is proud of the way he or she has packaged it. Nice, neat, and tidy and presented in a way that no one will know...or will they? If you are aware and intone with such things, I believe you can pick up some clues.

Yes, humility, like other things, can be contrived. If you learn the right language—how to respond to people, speak certain phrases or a have a certain tonality in your voice—you can learn how to "practice" humility. You can learn how to sound humble. Pulled off the right way, humility can catch the attention and focus of others. Some people wear their humility like a badge of honor.

Self-deprecation—people making fun of themselves or putting themselves down; especially done in a humorous way—is a pretty appealing thing. One of the books I have on public speaking actually recommends that you use some self-deprecating humor. I have personally used self-deprecating humor, but I have a friend and mentor who told me not to do that because I actually do occasionally put myself down and believe what I say about myself. Honestly, I don't know why I do this, if I do it because it looks good (people are attracted by it) or because I really believe it. It's probably because it looks like I'm humble, and that kind of humility really looks good. Ultimately, it's probably both because I have discovered that I have a Pharisee in Me, and I always have to be on the look-out for it to raise it's ugly head.

> If you learn the right language—how to respond to people, speak certain phrases or a have a certain tonality in your voice—you can learn how to "practice" humility.

> Humility is not something that you "do"; rather, it's something that you are.

Once again, I believe that humility is not something that you "do"; rather, it's something that you are. You can "be" humble, because the Holy Spirit has worked in your life in such a way that you "are" humble. But trying to be humble is very difficult without it being contrived. Such was the case of the incident when I said that I felt "unworthy"—which is a great buzz word for humility—

apparently in the way and manner that I said it, it sounded fake and contrived.

What makes humility fake and what makes it genuine? When are you being authentic, and when are you proud of your humility? These are questions with which everyone should struggle (even better is to use the study guide and are working this through with a study group). I do know this: some people work way too hard at trying to be humble, while others just are. One is Pharisaical, the other is genuine. One is packaging, the other is totally unaware of the package. One is proud of their humility, the other is surprised that they are even being humble. Because, if you are genuinely humble, I'm not sure that you know that you are.

Woe #7: Killing the Prophet (Matthew 23:29-36)

"Woe to you, teachers of the law and Pharisees, you hypocrites! You build tombs for the prophets and decorate the graves of the righteous. And you say, 'If we had lived in the days of our forefathers, we would not have taken part with them in shedding the blood of the prophets.' So you testify against yourselves that you are the descendants of those who murdered the prophets. Fill up, then, the measure of the sin of your forefathers!

"You snakes! You brood of vipers! How will you escape being condemned to hell? Therefore I am sending you prophets and wise men and teachers. Some of them you will kill and crucify; others you will flog in your synagogues and pursue from town to town. And so upon you will come all the righteous blood that has been shed on earth, from the blood of righteous Abel to the blood of Zechariah son of Berekiah, whom you murdered between the temple and the altar. I tell you the truth, all this will come upon this generation."

Part of being Pharisaical is making sure that you have few opponents. Speaking against the Pharisees was tantamount to speaking against God. After all, how could you challenge someone who is so holy, pure, righteous, and knowledgeable? Those who speak against them are obviously rebellious, arrogant, and insubordinate. While we will talk about this extensively in chapter on *"Blind Guides"* *the* issue at hand here is how we Pharisees get rid of or ostracize those who don't fit into our group or church; or those who go against the grain. (The truth is that everyone has an "agenda")

Although today we don't literally "kill" the prophet; we do find ways of not listening to them. Rather than listen, or engage in debate and dialogue we "kill" the messenger. For those who don't conform to our way of thinking or preaching, we point out how God wants "unity" and to "be of one mind". For fear of being critical, we no longer engage in critical thinking. We are told that those who have "their own agenda" are dangerous and not to be associated with, for they disrupt the ministry…how dare they! As David Johnson and Jeff VanVonderen comment, "[Likewise], those in spiritual positions of authority can violate our trust. It's possible to become so determined to defend a spiritual place of authority, a doctrine or a way of doing things that you wound and abuse anyone who questions, or disagrees, or doesn't "behave" spiritually the way you want them to." [6]

Jesus said, "no prophet is accepted in his hometown" (Luke 4:24, NIV). Or as other versions say, "a prophet is not honored in his own country". Why did he say that? What was his point? The concept of "not honored" relates to the idea

> Think alike, talk alike, and don't rock the boat and you'll be fine.

of not listening to, or not really hearing someone; not recognizing that what they are saying has worth or value. But for most of us, the practice of "not honoring" is not quite so blatant, rather, takes on more subtle forms. In fact, patronizing has become an art form. When we listen to someone, nod our heads, but don't really hear them…we're good at that!

Famous prophets are honored, but not those we know and are familiar with. You hear Bill Hybels, Rick Warren, Billy Graham, or Chuck Swindoll say something controversial and we consider their challenging statements as "exhorting"; but if we hear someone we don't know, or worse yet, someone we know only too well(in your church fellowship) say something against the grain and they are put off outright. They may even be told that they are being disruptive and rebellious. Never mind that they may have said the same thing the honored prophets said.

In the organizational world we call this "group think." To be a successful Pharisee you have to be "on the same page" and be speaking the same language. Think alike, talk alike, and don't rock the boat and you'll be fine. Better yet, when challenged, be in denial.

I once gave a pastor of a church a couple of challenging, "against the grain" books that I felt he should consider in thinking about the mood and direction of a particular church. After reading one of the books, he said, "I don't see anything in that that relates to our church." This is the problem with Pharisees: they read or hear something that pushes a little on their own security and they ignore its relevancy or think "that's for someone else (or some other church), but not my (or our) problem." But Pharisees kill the prophet by ignoring the message based upon who the messenger is. If they don't think the messenger carries any "weight" within their evangelical kingdom, if it has been determined that he or she "has their own agenda," the message will be considered irrelevant. Such, I believe, was the case in this instance.

This is perhaps easier to see in the world of politics. Within the United States we are now so polarized politically that we no longer talk to each other; rather, we try to subvert the other side even before they speak. If a Democrat knows that it is a Republican speaking he or she will begin to discount what they are about to say even before they speak, and visa versa. There are few from either side who are actually able to listen, discuss and debate with the other side.

Debates are no longer debates; rather they are barrages of half-truths, misunderstandings, innuendos and *ad hominem* arguments talking over each other; attacking the person, associating him or her with some clearly evil person from past history.   Tag someone with a label that will alienate them with your group and you will be successful in "killing the prophet."

One of the common things I appreciate about an institution such as Fuller Theological Seminary and my own pastor is the ability to co-exist with various viewpoints. The hearing, listening, and considering of other viewpoints isn't just patronizing, it's real. For example, my own pastor and I meet on a regular basis. He not only hears what I have to say, but considers things I say even if they are contrary to his own position or direction. We have within our church a wide collection of people who come from a diverse set of theological backgrounds; yet we are fairly unified. I attribute this to his sense of "hearing the prophet" rather than dissociating himself from those who don't agree with everything he says.

Fuller seminary is probably the most eclectic evangelical seminary in the nation. Certainly there are problems with this; yet there are opportunities as well. A couple years ago, asking the president of Fuller, Richard Mouw, how he could co-exist with such divergent positions within the same seminary; he said that he in fact was energized by it. There is wisdom here, because how are you ever supposed to hear prophetic words if you are surrounded with only those who come at things—and theology—from the same approach.

Hopefully, by now, everyone has seen that within the concepts of various kinds of Pharisees, and a variety of traits and tendencies of Pharisees, that they can identify how easy it is to become a Pharisee without really trying! However, there are still a few bases we need to cover in order to be prepared to rid ourselves of these self-righteous tendencies. We now need to discover false paradigms and concepts that we use to box ourselves into a Pharisaical corner. It is handling these misconceptions and identifying them for what they are that can become corrective measures in our life and within our church fellowship.

Chapter 8

Dismantling Pharisaical Mind-Sets
Understanding how misunderstood Scriptures create Pharisaical Attitudes.

"It is for freedom that Christ has set us free, stand firm, then, and do not let yourselves be burdened again by a yoke of slavery." Galatians 5:1

Stumbling over the 'stumbling block'

One of the most common reasons people fall into the trap of the Pharisaical Lure comes from misunderstanding certain portions of Scripture, which consequently leads to legalistic practices. Believe it or not, the 'stumbling block' Scriptures found primarily in Romans 14 and 1 Corinthians 8 contribute to more pharisaical 'requirements' than virtually any New Testament Scripture today. What we are about to talk about I call: *Being a Pharisee while trying to be considerate.*

First, let me quote the two verses that summarize what I'm talking about.

"All food is clean, but it is wrong for a man to eat anything that causes someone else to stumble" (Rom. 14:20). "Be careful, however, that the exercise of your freedom does not become a stumbling block to the weak" (1 Cor. 8:9.) The contemporary thinking that follows these verses is while

96

certain things are "allowed" they may not edify or build up the body. Worse yet, these things may "offend" some or even worse, cause someone to "stumble". The problem is that what these "things" are typically fall into a couple of categories. What it means to "stumble" is generally assumed, and misunderstood.

The categories that are usually attached to these stumbling block verses are drinking, clothing, and going to certain movies. The reasoning follows that while it may be okay to have a drink, for those who struggle with drinking it will offend them and cause them to stumble (if they see you have a drink). While it may be okay for women to wear skirts, it is better if they wear long dresses; knowing that their skirt may cause a man to lust, thus stumble. And while going to an R-rated move my certainly be alright, if others see you going into an 'R' movie you are encouraging them to do the same; at which time they might see something that will cause them to stumble; and on and on it goes.

These categories are usually generalized like this because they are easy targets, and few ever challenge someone holding to the stumbling block legalisms to take their argument to its logical conclusion. If you press the issue of what a stumbling block is you need to include other potentially "offensive" behavior. Such issues may then include things like:

- Wearing a particular kind of clothing to church
- Going to church on Sunday would be offensive to Seventh Day Adventists
- Going out to eat on Sunday would be offensive to those who believe that you are not supposed to make someone work on the Sabbath such as our Nazarene brothers and sisters and others within the holiness realm.
- The car you drive, the house you live in may be considered worldly 'trappings' by those who are more pious and tend toward "sacrificial" giving...having only the basics and giving all of their money to the poor or to missionaries.

- And a million other things which may "offend" someone. In short, there is probably something you do within your lifestyle that "offends" someone.

What constitutes a stumbling block?

It's bad enough that we reduce "offenses" to the select few items of spiritual acceptability, but the real culprit in this misunderstanding revolves around the concept of a stumbling block. If you read the context of the stumbling block Scriptures you will find that a stumbling block is a lot more egregious than something that merely "offends" someone.

> A stumbling block is a lot more egregious than something that merely "offends" someone.

In fact it is something so bad that it actually causes havoc or ruin of a person's faith. It is something so powerful that it could prevent someone from coming into the faith. Something that could cause a person to dissociate with the Christian faith because of a particular practice.

In order to get the feel of this, all you have to do is look at key words that surround this concept. In Romans 14 for example you will find words such as "grieved", "destroy", and "fall." Or in 1 Corinthians 8:7-13 you find the words, "defile" and "perish". The Amplified version uses words such as "defiled," "unholy," "injured," "cause ruin," "undo—breakdown—destroy [the work of God]," "give impulse [to sin] ," "tripped up," and "emboldened [to sin]." Wow! Those are heavy words!

Now connect these words within the typical assumptions. This would mean that if one Christian who believed it was "wrong" for a Christian to drink, saw another Christian have a drink that they would be so disillusioned by that act that they would be defiled and destroyed! If a Christian who believes it is 'wrong' for a Christian to go to R rated movies saw another brother or sister walk into one of those movies their faith would be wiped out! If a Christian woman who believes another [young] woman should not walk around with a bare midriff, saw someone who professes to be a Christian in that type of clothing, they would no longer be able to hold their faith together!

In the Romans 14 passage, the Geneva Study Bible, suggests that the word means, "to cut off from the covenant community", or "to encourage (weak) Christians to do what their conscious does not allow." William Barclay in *The Daily Study Bible* also identifies that this Scripture utilizes fairly strong terms. In his translation of this Scripture he writes that someone would be "*grieved* by something which you eat" and not to "*bring ruin* by what you eat to that man for whom Christ died."[1] [emphasis mine]

The key idea here is that the "strong" Christian persuades or influences a 'weak' Christian to do something that *causes* the person to sin to a point of *giving up on their faith*. (please note, I am not saying that a person can lose their faith, for I am a person who believes in eternal security, so don't be confused by these references to falling away— but that is for another discussion in another format). What I believe the context is here is either a new seeker who is closely investigating the faith and considering a commitment; or someone who is so disturbed by the particular "act" that they backslide. They may lose their passion, and never show up to fellowship and hear the word anymore because the gravity and the degree of the offensive is that it would cause this person to be so disillusioned that they are virtually "destroyed."   This could also apply if we would say that a strong Christian persuaded a weak Christian to do something that was "against their faith." Almost like someone persuading someone to deny Christ.   The point is that this "offense" is something much greater than being "offended." It is an offensive of great magnitude. It is an obstacle that keeps them from living their faith out in real life.

The Reverse Stumbling Block

One of the things seldom considered in the usage of these Scriptures is what I call a reverse stumbling block.

Those that create a legalistic atmosphere and requirements that come out of the thought process that they may "offend" someone are actually "offending" others who may feel no sense of shame or sin in the actions they do that "offend" the other. What do I mean?

You can actually create an atmosphere of legalism while trying to be "considerate" of those who may be "offended" by certain actions. In the DVD you will recall Joe Pharisee wanted everyone in his congregation to wear sandals and that tennis shoes were not acceptable. We could say that he didn't want to "offend" anyone who believed that sandals made of sacrificial leather were honoring to God and that tennis shoes were dishonoring to him. So to avoid "offending" those people he required everyone to wear sandals. But what of those who wear tennis shoes as part of their everyday garb? What about those who feel tennis shoes are fashionable and appropriate? Aren't they also offended by the implication that they aren't spiritual enough if they show up in tennis shoes? In fact they may feel more than uncomfortable in a church with an atmosphere like this. They may feel uptight, judged, belittled, and unacceptable. With an atmosphere like this, would it be any surprise that the tennis shoe wearers of the world simply wouldn't be interested in a Christianity that looked down upon them and denied them the feeling that they could be good Christians and wear tennis shoes too?

Those that advocate that it is wrong, offensive and a "stumbling block" to drink alcohol may create a system within their church which communicates that while the Bible doesn't necessarily doesn't forbid drinking, it is better not to so that you don't cause those who have problems with alcohol to stumble. Thus, as we discussed earlier, the abstinence of alcohol becomes the spiritual standard, and those who

> You can actually create an atmosphere of legalism while trying to be "considerate" of those who may be "offended" by certain actions.

"drink" are frowned upon, scorned, and cajoled, preached at, and guilt-ridden with suggestions that they must give it up if they are going to be obedient servants.

But what of those who not only appreciate a fine wine, but serve it in their restaurants? I happen to live in the wine country of southern California. Within a couple miles of my home are about 15 wineries. What of the owners of these wineries, can they embrace the claims of Christ upon their life and still own and operate their wineries? How would they feel if they walked into one of these churches? Would not the stumbling block *for them* be the suggestion that real Christians (or certainly highly spiritual and sacrificial Christians) don't drink? How about those who own and operate fine restaurants…is the young Christian, seeker, or even mature Christian for that matter, to think that they shouldn't serve wine or beer in their establishment if they are to be faithful to Christ and to the Christian community?

A fine Christian leader recently commented that this perspective is an "American issue". He spent three years in Australia and not only do they *not* have a problem with this, but many even bring wine to church gatherings! Are the Australian Christians wrong, sinful, and stumbling blocks while the American Christians who promote abstinence (from alcohol) right, more spiritual, and more holy?

> The reverse stumbling block however, is something few understand and even fewer churches acknowledge…

The reverse stumbling block however, is something few understand and even fewer churches acknowledge because they have done a good job of eliminating or keeping away from their fellowships those that are offended by their purified and sterile environments. In other words, in their very attempts to make their church members "holy", "pure", and clean of any stumbling block in their lives, they have unwittingly created a stumbling block in reverse. In essence they see it as their job not only to convert people to Christ but to make sure that they are the right type of Christian. As

John Fischer comments, "But Pharisees want more than control over the definition of sin. They want control of the holy things themselves. They set themselves up as the holy ones who have the inside track on God. They want people to come to them to get to God. This has always been the great temptation of spiritual position outside of the grace of God." [2]

So what do people do who are "offended" by these "non-offensive standards"? They stay away from them, and often from Christ. This is exactly what Jesus was talking about in the Seven Woes and exactly with the Pharisaical problem of "Kingdom Repellers" in Matthew 23:13. Oh, to have our churches designed around the concept of grace! But wait; do we perpetuate too much grace?

Too much grace (or, Grace is good, but law is better)

I recently had a discussion with someone who was defending a noted leader, whom I inadvertently called "legalistic". Now, I have to admit, that it was probably a knee jerk reaction on my part, and in the process I am probably guilty of being a Pharisee about Pharisees. I am judging the judger.

But in his exuberance to defending this noted leader, he jumped into the discussion with what he called "his passion." The discussion focused on the fact that he felt that too many evangelicals were emphasizing grace too much. "Grace, grace, that's all they talk about!" was his criticism. No one wants to talk about obedience which God demands; everyone wants to focus on His grace. We are told to obey his commands and we need to know what they are so that we can obey them. "People think that because of his grace they can live how they want...that his commands aren't important."

In fact there is a statement of Augustine's which I often quote, "Love God, and live how you want." Line drawers and command bearers can't handle a statement like this. It's too loose. It's too vague. It doesn't define our boundaries, and doesn't let us know what we are commanded to *do*; it doesn't let us know what *you* need to do, and if I know what you need to do, then I can make sure you tow that line! After all, didn't Jesus give us commands? He didn't just die to let us live how we want...isn't that "cheap grace"?

The reference to "cheap grace" comes from Dietrich Bonhoeffer's classic book, *The Cost of Discipleship*, which takes up the subject of what God's grace does to us and for us, and our response to His grace, the question being, "What is our life to be like because of His grace which was so costly?" His answer is a life of discipleship, and then attempts to explain what that looks like. His contrasts between cheap and costly grace are forever challenging words that should ring in all of our ears. He says:

> Cheap grace is grace without discipleship, grace without the cross, grace without Jesus Christ, living and incarnate. Costly grace is the treasure hidden in the field; for the sake of it a man will gladly go and sell all that he has. It is the pearl of great price to buy which the merchant will sell all his goods. It is the kingly rule of Christ, for whose sake a man will pluck out the eye which causes him to stumble, it is the call of Jesus Christ at which the disciple leaves his nets and follows him....Such grace is costly because it calls us to follow, and it is grace because it calls us to follow Jesus Christ. It is costly because it costs a man his life, and it is grace because it gives a man the only true life. It is costly because it condemns sin and grace because it justifies the sinner. Above all, it is costly because it cost God the life of his Son: "ye were bought with a price" and what cost God much cannot be cheap for us...
>
> Costly grace confronts us as a gracious call to follow Jesus; it comes as a word of forgiveness to the broken spirit and the

contrite heart. Grace is costly because it compels a man to submit to the yoke of Christ and follow him; it is grace because Jesus says: "My yoke is easy and my burden is light."[3]

But what most people don't know, that Georg Huntemann points out in his book, *The Other Bonhoeffer*, is that Bonhoeffer apparently noticed a "backlash" from his book which created a kind of super-spiritual Christianity; one that focuses on religiosity, something actually contrary to what he set out to do. Huntemann points out that in Bonhoeffer's *Letters and Papers from Prison*, which occurred much later in his life, he reflects upon this, in the following way: "I thought I could acquire faith by trying to live a holy life, or something like it. I suppose I wrote *The Cost of Discipleship* as the end of that path. Today I can see the dangers of that book, though I still stand by what I wrote."[4]

> Bonhoeffer would not contradict what he wrote but seemed to feel that people took it the wrong way. This goes to the question of the guy who says we flaunt God's grace, or treat it "cheaply". And it goes to the question of Paul who asked (rhetorically) in Romans 6:1, "What shall we say, then? Shall we go on sinning so that grace may increase?" (NIV) Dialoguing with himself, as he was dialoguing with us, Bonhoeffer reveals the tension between these two worlds:

> Did not even Luther speak of *pecca fortiter* (sin bravely), so that the Christian, all the more lively and joyful in his faith in God's love, can become certain of God's grace to him, even though he is a sinner? Cannot one then be carefree and "sin with impunity while Christ foots the bill"? ...For Luther,

pecca fortiter can only be "the consolation for one whose attempts to follow Christ had taught him that he can never become sinless, who in his fear of sin despairs of the grace of God... those who from the bottom of their hearts make a daily renunciation of sin and of every barrier which hinders him from following Christ, but who nevertheless are troubled by their faithlessness and sin. [5]

We have here an ultimate paradox. It's only in realizing that we are sinners, and that we can never do away with our sin; and only when we humbly and daily come before God and ask His forgiveness that we are able to live without worrying about our sin. Bonhoeffer, it appears, detested attempts at "obedience" done out of a motivation to become "holy" in the sense of personally righteous; and further the attempts which causes the Christian to go into his holy huddle of spiritual confines that keeps his Christianity out of relevancy to his real life and the real world. He says,

Cheap grace is religion....Neither does a disciple of Christ run himself down through a kind of whiny self-pity about his sinfulness. Discipleship is not a self-fixated, egocentric perseverance, but a joyful, trusting, steady progression. Discipleship is not self-pitying. Rather, it trusts in forgiveness. Grace does not inhabit merely a corner of the world, but dwells in the midst of life. [6]

The irony of all this is that obedience to Christ and cross bearing is not that we retreat to the confines of our Christian fellowships to become "holy other." That is, not that cross bearing is becoming super-spiritual; rather, obedience, costly grace, and discipleship is lived out in the real world, with real people, with real problems; and *with* us we bring the grace of Jesus Christ.

105

This leads me to discuss Galatians 5:1, which I use as the cornerstone verse for *Reality Check Resources*: "It is for freedom that Christ has set us free, stand firm, then, and do not let yourselves be burdened again by a yoke

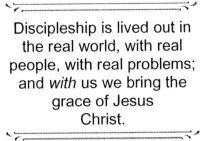

Discipleship is lived out in the real world, with real people, with real problems; and *with* us we bring the grace of Jesus Christ.

of slavery."   The yoke of slavery here that Paul is talking about is the tendency to always to want to go back to the law to please God. It is the feeling deep inside that says, "Grace is good, but law is better". But the law binds us up and becomes religiosity, which is nothing other than self-righteous standard-bearing, line-drawing, yoke-imposing pharisaicalism. Instead, Jesus wants to free us up to live life for in within the context of the world he put us in.

Rather than be bound by a yoke of slavery, we are bound by grace, and free to live life grace-fully, which is a subject we will pick up again in the last chapter.

The "holding people accountable" issue

But doesn't the Bible tell us we are to hold our brother accountable? Aren't we supposed to exercise discipline within our churches? Isn't it our responsibility to keep our churches pure? Aren't you advocating relativism? Well, before I go much further, perhaps

But anytime we are making public the sin of another in an effort to "hold them accountable" we run the risk of" bearing false witness" against them.

it might be a tip off that those who are "really concerned" about the answer to these questions are already inflicted with a Pharisaical attitude and questions like these reinforce these attitudes. On the other hand, they are legitimate questions because the Bible does teach we are to hold each other accountable, but I believe it is within a certain realm or context. "Discipline" isn't a regular occurrence within the life of the church but should be rare and extreme. While I will talk about the discipline issue in the section on *Blind Guides*, I do want to address the accountability issue here, with it's dangers and when and how "accountability" is to take place.

One of the dangers of the "accountability" question is "bearing false witness against our neighbor." This issue was brought to my attention a couple years ago in a meeting I had with a prominent seminary professor. It is a perspective that I had not even considered before. Whenever I had previously read or referred to the Ten Commandments and read the command not to "bear false witness" I never considered it to be something I ever had to deal with or worry about. "Bearing false witness," I thought, solely referred to a kind of courtroom situation where I was committing perjury against someone; not telling the truth about them in a way that harmed them legally. Somehow, I never considered it's implications in everyday life.

But anytime we are making public the sin of another in an effort to "hold them accountable" we run the risk of "bearing false witness" against them. First of all, we need to be absolutely sure that the "sin" for which we are holding someone accountable is an actual sin. Then we need to be absolutely sure that the sin was committed. Opinions, feelings, not liking what someone is doing and even "concern" do not constitute a justifiable accountability issue. If someone is being a stumbling block about issues we previously talked about—issues which really don't fall into the sin category—and you think you are holding them accountable for such an issue, you may be "bearing false witness" against them and you may also be a stumbling block to them in reverse. In the process you have *judged* them, even judged them in the presence of others, even up-lined this false witness of them to your own spiritual leaders (your pastors and elders) as you reported to them their evil deeds.

This kind of judging reeks of condemnation and the overwhelming ability to make ourselves look good while looking down on others. As Dallas Willard says:

> We have great confidence in the power of condemnation to "straighten others out." And if that fails, should we not at least make clear that we are on the side of the right—no small matter itself?...When we condemn another we really communicate that he or she is, in some deep and just possibly irredeemable way, bad—bad as a whole, and to be rejected...Condemnation always involves some degree of self-righteousness and of distancing ourselves from the one we are condemning. And self-righteousness always involves an element of comparison and of condemnation. Jesus spoke to "some who were relying upon themselves for their rightness and were despising others" (Luke 18:9).[7]

The accountability issue is a slippery slope and one we need to be extremely careful of. I know of a middle aged couple who were cast under such judgment by the "concern" and "accountability" of someone in their fellowship. The wife of this couple shared with several of her Christian friends, within the confines of confidentiality, how God had worked in her marriage. She talked about some of the problems they had experienced in their marriage in such a way that from her tonality and the way she shared, it seemed like the problems may still be present. Her intent was that they needed to understand how difficult things had been (in the past). These issues were not obvious to these women because the couple had gone through these problems years before. But the issues were surprising to the others because the couple in question were leaders in the church. Unfortunately, shocked by the story, one of these women was sure something was wrong in their current marriage, something so wrong she felt she had to express her "concern" to someone in higher spiritual authority.

The woman was so concerned that one of her leaders wasn't 'whole' or that there was something wrong (sin?) that she "shared" this "problem" with the wife of the Associate Pastor of that church. The wife in turn shared it with her husband; who in turn, went over to this couple's home to confront them with their "problem" (sin?).

The couple tried to explain to the pastor that it was a misunderstanding; the ladies simply didn't understand that this was an issue from the past. Unfortunately, the damage had been done because the pastor refused to accept that it was only in the past, but chose to believe that it was still something present in their marriage. He based his conclusion on two "facts." First, he had checked with one other woman to whom this story was told (there were three altogether) if she felt there was a current problem in this couple's marriage. Since she also concurred, he was sure it was not a misunderstanding but that something was "there." Secondly, he explained that a couple of years before this woman (wife) had shared with his wife a similar thing, that there were "problems" within their marriage. Although he really didn't know what current problems existed, he was convinced that there "was something there."

I tell this story because bearing false witness and gossip often fall under the guise of concern and accountability. Being the super-spiritual people that they were (Pharisees?), they needed to set this couple right, and be sure that they weren't damaging the ministry. This pastor not only supported the "false witness" and gossip of this other person, but asked the couple to no longer lead the home group they had lead for four years!

I personally know this pastor, he is a good guy, he truly loves the Lord, and most importantly has had a real impact on people within the church he serves. His church is a good church, a dynamic and growing church that is changing lives for Christ. The point I am making here is not that this pastor is bad, but that he is no better than the couple who were being confronted and being "held accountable." The "holding others accountable" issue has been misused, misunderstood, and been exercised by many sincere and "concerned" Christians to make right what was never wrong in the first place. That is to say, wrong to the point of sin, enough to be a stumbling block, or sin enough to destroy a person's faith, or sin enough to destroy a ministry. Oh, and about that couple: they left that church for another; they are still growing and thriving in their marriage, and affecting people for Christ. They are still however, the same people.

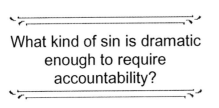

What kind of sin is dramatic enough to require accountability?

This, then, begs the question, how much sin is enough sin? What kind of sin is dramatic enough to require accountability? At what point is accountability okay? Well, to fully unpack questions like these we need to break it down to the least common denominator. Start with the absurd or extreme case and then work your way backward to more "normal" instances. Expose the issue in such a way that if you carry the thought through to its logical conclusion you will discover how ridiculous or silly it might be.

If a person is "caught" lusting, should they be confronted and "held accountable"? If so, when, and how often? After the first look? After every look? Whoever doesn't lust, cast the first stone. What about having "problems" in a marriage; does a marriage have to be absent of problems and struggles for it to be considered spiritual or holy enough for a couple to minister to others? Whoever doesn't have problems in their marriage, cast the first stone. What about problems with anger; should someone who gets angry be "held accountable" and confronted with each occurrence? He who never gets angry, cast the first stone.

What about gossip, bad language, disagreement, overeating, driving over 55, eating too many carbs, coming in late for church, not coming to church every Sunday, etc. Do all of these inconsistencies, delinquencies, fallacies, and stumblings that are part of our everyday life require and call for accountability? Is this not just another aspect of "sin management"? Is it the *responsibility* of a more mature 'godly' person to confront and hold accountable anybody and everybody within the body for any and every sin…or perceived sin…or "concern"? These are the questions we need to wrestle with, but in attempting to answer them, they raise even more questions.

The biggest problem with all this is that there are no neat and tidy answers. For example, probably the key Scripture everyone uses in the accountability issue is Matthew 18:15-20; which talks about what to do when a brother sins against you. This Scripture is also often used in cases of church discipline. Most see it as a three step process in how to hold someone accountable for their sin.

But if you look for an explanation in William Barcley's commentary, *The Daily Study Bible*, he points out that there is much confusion surrounding this portion of Scripture. Some of the questions I have (which I mentioned above) are: What kind of sin is being referred to here? What is the degree of sin? Isn't this a "sin" in which one person does damage to another person? When it talks about taking the issue to the "church" if the person doesn't repent of their sin, and if the sinner doesn't "heed" or "listen" to the church then they are to treat this person as tax collectors or gentiles; it evokes even more curiosity: Didn't Jesus hang out with tax collectors and gentiles? In fact, didn't he tell the Pharisees that these sinners would be more welcome within the kingdom than they? What of the woman about to be stoned by the self-righteous Pharisees; didn't Jesus say to them that whoever was without sin cast the first stone?—the result being that they walked away and Jesus saying, "…and neither do I condemn you, go and sin [that sin] no more." What of Peter's three time denial of Jesus? Why was he so easily forgiven…even given a position of prominence? Why wasn't he put on probation for a period of two, or five years? These are nagging questions, with anything but crystal clear answers. However, there are some insights that take most of these questions "off the table." Those insights will come in a moment.

Accounting for accountability

For now, let me provide a few guidelines when accountability *is* acceptable and when it *is* our responsibility:

First, if someone has specifically asked you to hold them accountable. This, of course, implies a real relationship exists. And this is not a manipulative attempt within a relationship to be spiritual overseers of each other. It is a common thing today to have men's groups and men meeting on a regular basis for the purpose of holding each other accountable. This is a good thing if it is really desired by the participants, rather than coerced by a manipulative leader or a nosy meddler.

There seems to be an indication that the older men were mentoring the younger and the older women mentoring the younger women. (Titus 2:2-4, 1 Peter 5:4-6). Being "accountable" within the context of a mentoring (discipleship) relationship takes on a whole different spirit then the idea of "setting someone right." I personally, have two older gentlemen with whom I meet with (individually) on a regular basis. I cherish their insight, guidance, encouragement, and sometimes "correction." I trust them both immensely with my hopes, dreams, thoughts, struggles, and occasionally a "sin" or temptation. I thank God for their wisdom, experience, love and care. So within a context like this, much can be accomplished, a person can grow, be continually restored, rejuvenated, directed and guided, always by a "truth in love" kind of atmosphere.

Secondly, when a clear and egregious sin has been committed by someone. But the question comes, how egregious is egregious? The sin mentioned in 1 Corinthians 5:1-13 for example, was the sin of incest. But more than that; it appeared to be a kind of "in your face" sin; done right in front of everyone (not the actual sin, but the evidence of it). There was an "I don't care if you know" attitude that seemed to be present, and a church fellowship had an "I don't care if you do" attitude.

Even then it is less an issue of "holding someone accountable" than it was an issue of restoring someone who may be struggling with a sin. It appears that 2 Corinthians 2:5-11 may refer to the same person who, after Paul's chastisement of the church, was then dealt with too harshly. And even if it wasn't the same person, we need to realize that restoration is the underlying spirit of the matter. Restoration is a tricky issue, especially within the life of the church. We seem more capable of shooting our wounded, than we are of restoration.

I only know of a few cases in which a man (or a woman) caught in adultery has been lovingly and carefully restored in their marriage *and* within their church. In these cases the pastors, elder board and people with counseling and nurturing gifts wrapped themselves around these couples to help them heal, and then subsequently re-engage themselves within the life of the church. Unfortunately, I know of more cases when such sin-committers are cast out, ostracized, talked about, and left to fend for themselves and wallow in the depth of their sin. Such is the case when leaders and church members no longer wanting to associate with a person mentally and emotionally abandon them to fend for themselves. This is a common tale, causing an estrangement from the church and in some cases estrangement from God.

2 Thessalonians 3:6, 14, 15 deals with those who refused to work, moochers, who were not ashamed of their idleness, but again "rubbed it in God's face," and in the face of the body of Christ. The Scripture says that they "walk disorderly" which seems to indicate that behind the actual sin, the "greater sin" (if there is such a thing) was defiance of God! It was an "in your face," "I don't care," no shame attitude! Paul ends his comments by saying that "if anyone does not obey our instruction in this letter…do not associate with him" (NIV). It is direct and clear disobedience, it is *defiance* of God, not man, which is the issue. It seems that the most egregious sins fall into that category, which we will turn to next.

Third, when there is a flat out defiance of God and the body of Christ concerning a SIN which affects the life and faith of another, even the entire church. This is where accountability turns into church discipline. But here is the thing that is most often NOT recognized: most of the stronger texts, which seem to support some type of church discipline, have to do with doctrine and truth, not lifestyle. It is within the context of false teaching, bad teaching, misleading teaching, false doctrine, and aberrant theology that we get stronger words from the likes of Paul. Scriptures often used for "accountability" issues and general church discipline such as Galatians 2:11, 12; 1 Timothy 1:20; 1 Timothy 5:20; 2 Timothy 2:14-26; Titus 1:10-16; and Titus 3:9-11 all deal with "truth and theology" issues. These Scriptures all have to do with false teachers messing with the minds of a very vulnerable and newly forming church. The biggest reaction actually coming against those who advocated a return to the law and legalistic practices!

When you read Titus 1, for example, the framework for an "elder" who should "not be guilty of insubordination" or, as the NIV says, not "wild and disobedient," the issue is about teaching and truth! Reading further in verses 10-16 you will find he is talking about: "subvert[ing] households," wrong and bad teaching, "dishonest gain," leaning on "commandments of men," and those who "turn from the truth."

Paul is actually referencing the Judaizers who were Jewish "converts" to Christianity, who wanted Gentile Christians to first be circumcised and adhere to Jewish ceremonial law before they were accepted as full-fledged Christians. Paul, in fact, in Galatians 2:1-3, refused to have Titus circumcised, confronted Peter to his face for going along with the idea (Gal. 2:11,12), and spoke of these misguided ones as "false brothers" (Gal. 2:4). Worse yet, he says in the

> Of all the things to worry about, to be "concerned" about, to hold others and the church "accountable" to, it is legalism.

beginning of Galatians, as he addressed the entire Galatian church, that anyone preaching a gospel of "law" or "legalism" is preaching a false gospel and they are "anathema" (NKJV) or "eternally condemned". He says, "You're going to hell if you keep this up!" "Get off it!" "Don't allow yourselves to go down that path!" Of all the things to worry about, to be "concerned" about, to hold others and the church "accountable" to, it is legalism. Legalism is the most detestable thing! It stinks of something that is anti-Christian, and anti-Christ!

Speaking of the Judaizers to the Galatian church in Galatians 3:1-3, Paul says that the Galatians are bewitched. Ken Blue points this out, saying:

> Calling the Galatians "bewitched" suggests that their false teachers are witches. "Bewitched" refers to "the evil eye," which was the primary mode of witchcraft in the Mediterranean world. The evil eye was a witch's spell that slowly sucked the life out of its victim (an apt description of legalism)....It is vital to remember that those who cast these life-sucking theological spells did not look like witches, even though they were. They looked instead like Pharisees: respected, highly disciplined and godly. Luther comments, "The holier the heretics seem to be, the more dangerous their cause." [8]

Now, to underline this, let's go back to the most often used Scripture of accountability which is the issue of one person "sinning against a brother" found in Matthew 18:15-20. There are two things to consider before finalizing any preset beliefs about what it means. First, forget the divisions we have made in our modern Bible and take it within the context of Matthew 18:21-35. The emphasis here is on forgiveness! How many times? _____ (you fill in the blank). Now, consider this: the number you have in your mind isn't high enough. If the one "holding someone accountable" doesn't in the end forgive; the monkey is on his or her back. The issue is about restoration of a relationship and forgiveness is part and parcel to that.

Secondly, Calvin has an interesting perspective on this matter. He points out that what is normally thought of as step number two, which is that if the person does not "repent" of their sin, then the person offended should bring in one or two "witnesses." In his commentary on the book of Matthew, regarding this issue he distinguishes between "denial" and "evasion. The denial here is not the kind I've previously talked about, where someone is "in denial." Rather, it is a case in which the person "declares that he is falsely accused." In this case, he says the person "must be left alone." In other words, if the person says, "you've got it wrong" or "you've misunderstood" or "that didn't happen," then BACK OFF! Don't press the issue, and don't involve other people in a sin that is not a sin! The issue of evasion of a sin is another thing altogether, and is what we normally would put in the category of being "in denial".

I don't believe that the "spirit" of the law of accountability is that we all become accountability cops in each others lives. Then what you will have is a situation in which we are not living life in the fullest, but living life defensively. Conditions like these will cause people to look over their shoulders, become insecure, uptight, and afraid that they might be doing something wrong in someone else's opinion. A Christian living under this kind of scenario lives an anxious, worrisome life; fearing that someone may think they are not living acceptably, that their approval rating may go down, and that their faith and fellowship may be threatened. Who knows when the next accountability cop will go to their pastor out of "concern" for a "sinning" brother and sister?

A healthier, non-pharisaical perspective is to consider what YOU are accountable to one another FOR; which is to: love (Jn 13:34), be devoted to (Rom. 12:10), be in harmony with (Rom. 12:16), accept (Rom. 15:7), instruct (Rom. 15:14), greet (Rom. 16:16),agree [unity not uniformity] (1

Cor. 1:10), serve (Gal. 5:13), be patient with (Eph. 4:2), be kind and compassionate toward (Eph. 4:30), bear with (Col. 3:13), teach and admonish (Col. 3:16), encourage (1 Thes. 5:11), spur on (Heb. 10:24), and to be in harmony with (1 Pet. 4:9). There is enough here for me to worry about doing for others, rather than worry about being the accountability cop for the body of Christ.

This leads us to discussing the matter of the Pharisaical systems set up by those in leadership, especially within a spiritual realm. The next concern we need to face is that of Pharisaical Leaders.

Chapter 9

Blind Guides

Four ways spiritual leaders become Pharisees

"You blind guides! You strain out a gnat but swallow a camel." Matthew 23:24

Now we must deal with the most difficult part of this entire subject. It is difficult simply because it deals with those who perpetuate the entire pharisaical program. This is difficult because these folks hold the power, are influential, have a platform, and hold "positions of authority." The very act of writing what I'm about to write could be considered threatening to those who "hold the power" within the church. I'm talking about pastors, elders, and leaders of local church congregations. On the other hand, every pastor/leader who reads this COULD be interested because they don't see that they may have this problem; which of course, could also be a case of denial.

But consider this: THE PHARISEES, SADDUCEES, SCRIBES, AND RABBIS were the spiritual leaders of the day. Who they were, and the function they filled, are represented in the pastors of today! But also consider: I have spent an entire book talking about how it is easy for

EVERYONE to become a Pharisee, including the pastors and elders of our local churches. So if you are a member of a local congregation, don't start this section with a sense of spiritual smugness; thinking (or saying), "See, they're the problem." And if you are a Pastor/leader within your congregation; don't think for one minute that I'm picking on you, or stirring up your congregation to work against you or your teaching. Pastors and leaders within our churches are to be held with the highest degree of respect and appreciation. They are to be loved and cared for, as they care for us. They are also to be respected— not worshiped; appreciated—not crowned with infallibility; cared for—not un- criticized. As we have seen earlier, we are not to be blindly devoted followers, nor should we promote such a thing.

The physical platform itself puts them "above" their people and that visual presence alone, week after week, provides a visual reinforcement of their "authority."

The issues I want to address, however, concern how Pharisaical systems are set up within our churches, and how pastors become the chief enablers of these systems. In turn, pastors and leaders "put themselves in Moses' seat" which makes them all powerful, and untouchable. This is not usually a conscious act, but is implicit within the very system and church culture that THEY set up.

Before we go any further, I think it will be helpful to review the working definition of a Pharisee:

I am a Pharisee when I set up precise standards or actions which I have determined equate to righteousness, holiness, and obedience; and judge others in relationship to my own ability to meet those standards [even when I use Scripture].

The question is: who sets up standards of righteousness? The answer is, we do, but even more so, those who lead their congregations do. As a CEO and president set the stage for the corporate culture to be developed, so the Pastor creates the standards which create the atmosphere for the culture of the particular church. Their platform, which in most cases is at the very least the Sunday sermon, and usually more, provides them constant visual and psychological power. The physical platform itself puts them "above" their people and that visual presence alone, week after week, provides a visual reinforcement of their "authority."

Even today, some pastors still wear a robe when preaching. The background of the robe, if I understand it correctly, had to do with the concept that when a Pastor put on a robe it was no longer them who the congregation should focus on, but God, that the words he was about to speak were, "thus saith the Lord." This is about 50% of a good idea. Like so many things, the original intention has not only lost it's meaning, but has the reverse effect. Robes on pastors can be construed as presumptuous, aloof, condescending, arrogant, ostentatious, and that the pastor is somehow untouchable. If you are a pastor and you are in a church and denomination in which robes are traditionally worn, I mean no offense; yet, I would highly recommend that you reflect upon and consider whether or not your robe wearing actually serves and benefits those to whom you serve and minister. Consider if it makes you seem real or unreal, aloof or connected to the real and everyday lives of those in your pews. I would strongly encourage you to examine the necessity of a robe.

Most pastors today have left the formalities behind and wear robes of other sorts. These new robes are protective garbs that create a perception of power and authority. The physical platform is one of these tools of authority which perpetuate this. The weekly sermon is another. (by the way, this is unavoidable…that's where the Pastor should be)

In this chapter I want to address other aspects of their new robes. These new robes are also four ways in which spiritual leaders of today can become Pharisees. They are:

- The "Don't touch me" aura

- The "I'm responsible for you" mind-set
- "Scriptural Intimidation" and control
- "Locked in" social undercurrents

All of these are self-reinforcing principles and overlap each other. It's all part of the robe. These four ways combined create a very powerful venue for a modern day Pharisee to rise unwittingly, unknowingly, and unintentionally out of any Christian leader today.

Don't touch me

This concept comes from two Biblical sources: one misconstrued the other brought to our attention by Jesus. The first is the idea perpetuated by the reference to "touch not the Lord's anointed." Consistent with robe wearing is the idea that the person underneath the robe can't be touched. It's a "hands off" feature of robes. A robe calls attention to the fact that underneath this garb is a special person, someone you should honor. It elevates the person to another realm, above and separate from those around who are wearing regular clothes. It is the envelope of protection, the hermetically sealed environment of an untouchable spirit projected by those who advocate this mistruth. Modern day Pharisees may not be cloistered within the confines of a monastery; rather, they hide behind the robe of mystical authority. I once heard a pastor say (about those who were challenging a direction his church was going), "It's a dangerous thing to go against God's ministry"! His implication: "How dare you challenge what we are doing here?!" Statements like these are robes of protection, and employ manipulation and coercion.

The concept of a special anointing is dangerous one, first because I don't believe it is Biblical; and second, because of everything a special anointing implies. A special anointing implies a special person, one who has a special, more spiritual, and more authoritative pronouncement. A special anointing implies a person who embodies the Words of God in ways which are to be feared or honored above others.

Ken Blue, in his poignant book, *Healing Spiritual Abuse* points out,

> This phrase, which comes from 1 Chronicles 16:22 and Psalm 105:15, is taken out of context and twisted to meet the need. When David uttered these words he was warning his men not to kill King Saul, whom the Lord himself had anointed with oil and the Holy Spirit....David's warning not to kill the king has nothing whatever to do with our treatment of church leaders today...the exclusive spiritual anointing that came upon the kings, prophets and priests in the Old Testament is now lavishly poured out on all God's people. To speak of anyone as especially anointed like the Old Testament leaders engages an exaggerated awe of that person. It also implies a class system in the kingdom of God, where no such system exists.[1]

As a side note to this, I want to differentiate between ordination and anointing. A healthy perspective of ordination would be to see it as someone who is set aside for a particular ministry. These people have a specific calling, and a specific task within the ministry of a congregation, but to say they have a special anointing goes too far. While no one within Protestantism would say that they are infallible, a special anointing implies an almost pope-like "command" over people. Who, after all, can argue or

> A special anointing implies an almost pope-like "command" over people. Who, after all, can argue or disagree with someone who has a special anointing? How could they possibly be wrong?

disagree with someone who has a special anointing? How could they possibly be wrong?

The special anointing concept merges well with what Jesus himself said about the Pharisees, that they "sit in Moses' seat" (Matt. 23:2). The seat of Moses was an actual stone-built chair that a rabbi or teacher would sit in outside the temple area. It was in itself a high platform and rose above the people so that the teacher could expound upon his teaching and answer questions to the audience below. If you look on this book cover, and especially see the DVD you will notice someone we have called Joe Pharisee. On the book cover and on the cover of all our materials you will see Joe standing on a mound, projecting the idea that he is above others. Better yet, if you watch the DVD in the opening scene you will see Joe walk out and literally sit in a seat that is far above those he is teaching. He is sitting in Moses' seat. Moses' seat was a seat of authority, a seat of position, a seat of teaching where those below would be amazed at the wisdom which would so eloquently be delivered to them from these learned men.

You don't challenge those in Moses seat. You listen, learn, and ask questions...but you don't challenge. And "how dare you if you do"! To challenge them was tantamount to challenging God: it was disrespectful and rebellious. Yet, interestingly enough we are reminded that Jesus spoke "to some who are confident of their own righteousness" (Luke 18:9), not to be so confident and intimidating with their knowledge.

A robe of righteousness is worn when there is a strong emphasis on "not touching the Lords anointed" and when someone "sits in Moses seat" proclaiming their spiritual superiority and authority over someone. This, of course, has long been a problem within the Christian church, a problem we can't seem to get away from. As the church distanced itself in time as an original and dynamic organism, it found itself increasingly falling into Pharisaical traps. The priesthood and the monastic movement underline the epitome of a twisted mind-set and moving the church from an organism to an institution. In spite of the rallying cry of

Peter that "you are a kingdom of priests" and the words of Paul that "you are all ministers," over time we kept misplacing a generalized spiritual authority to a specific one; from everyone equally under the authority of the Word of God…to a person specifically appointed to impart His Word—in other words, a priest. A big part of the battle of the reformers was to go against the power system embodied within the clergy; in their case, the Roman Catholic Church and the hierarchical and bureaucratic structure they set up. Protestants have typically believed that they have left that concept behind, emphasizing that there is no mediator between God and man, save Jesus Christ Himself. But, over the years, an unbalanced view continues to creep up, and the idea of a priesthood of a specific person, although not referred to that as such, has taken office within the pastorate and the person preaching the Word from the pulpit week in and week out. In other words, the pastor is still looked upon and treated as if he was a priest specific, with a more direct connection with God and His Word than the average, everyday believer.

In the denomination I grew up in, for which I still have a great love even though I no longer am a member; there was a special reference to the minister. The *Dominie*, as he was referred to, was a Dutch connotation (although of Latin origin) that seemed to refer to someone who had a high and holy calling. It referred to someone who was to be revered. And revered he was, to the point that it seemed like he had one foot in heaven and one foot on earth. There was an aura that surrounded him and a sense of awe that was projected toward him. Never really totally here, but someone who was up there…in the spiritual highlands…far from where I lived.

The danger here that is always lurking is that whether it is a reference to "touch not the Lord's anointed," any symptom or representation of a pastor/teacher "sitting in Moses' seat," or even a concept like the Dutch one of a Domanie, the result is always the same: a misappropriated sense of authority from God's Word, to a specific person. This violation is subtle and dangerous. But make no mistake: it happens within our evangelical churches every day.

As Michael Horton exhorts in his book, *Power Religion*:

> Authority is derived from the Word, not from the office. If the minister is not faithful to the word and to the gospel it proclaims, he is a usurper. There is no such thing as "the Lord's anointed," preachers who are above the Word with whose protection they are entrusted. Any claim to divine authority for commands, expectations, "revelations," or guidance that are not stated in the pages of Holy Scripture are marks of a spiritual tyrant and Pharisee.[2]

I'm Responsible for You

The next robe of self-righteousness adorned by those in power is the concept that they are responsible for us…for you and for me. Once again, this is not wholly wrong. It is partly true. We are told to "Obey your leaders and submit to their authority. They keep watch over you as men who must give an account." (Hebrews 13:17). You might think: "what's unclear about that?" The lack of clarity comes from misunderstanding the concept of authority, submission on our part and the accounting on their part. The concept is really more about their responsibility to serve and ours to willingly follow. Their service, the way they teach, and the way they lead should cause us to follow willingly. It is not submission against our will, but a matter of following because we see from their manner that they are leading in a way which will build up the body of Christ. It's not a demanded or assumed authority, but a followed one.

None-the-less, there is confusion surrounding the concepts of obedience, authority, and how far a pastor's responsibility extends and followership. Commenting on this misunderstood issue of submission and followership David

Johnson and Jeff VanVonderen say, "...Scripture verses quickly come to mind in seeming support of a blind sort of obedience and submission. (such as, Heb 13:7, Rom. 13:1,2) Why? Because he's the pastor, that's why. This type of thinking is a symptom of living under leadership that legislates and demands obedience to their authority. It rests upon a false basis of authority."[3]

For example Hebrews 13:17 says, "Obey your leaders and submit to their authority. They keep watch over you as men who must give an account. Obey them so that their work will be a joy, not a burden, for that would be of no advantage to you." (NIV) Commenting on this Scripture Ken Blue points out,

> To begin with, this verse does not apply to any leader who does not function first of all as a servant "watching over" the followers. Second, the New Testament word here for "obey" (*peithomai*) does not refer to the obedience that may be demanded by right or imposed by decree. Rather, this kind of trust is given voluntarily to leaders in response to their character and the power of their persuasion.[4]

But the temptation to become Pharisaical is stronger and easier within the pastorate and leadership of local churches precisely because of all the props available to them. The robes of self-righteousness are almost built into their office and function. Because of this there is a tremendous need to be aware of and fight these temptations.

My own pastor is an amazing servant of the Lord. He is a man of compassion, consistency, and giving of himself and of his time. As of this writing I have met with him every other week for about three years now, and he never ceases to amaze me. I willingly follow him because I know his thought process, I know how he makes decisions, and I know that he puts himself last in making decisions that are good for our church. More importantly, what keeps him from abusing his office is that he sincerely listens. He takes into serious consideration things that I have brought to his attention. He especially considers those things I have talked about that go "against" or are contrary to his position. And all the while I have never, ever felt that he looked down upon me, or that he was disturbed because I was somehow disrupting the unity of the church. I will follow this man as long as that spirit is within him, which I'm pretty sure will be until the Lord takes him.

On the other hand, you may recall the story of the pastor of which I told you in the previous chapter who seemed to advocate gossip and under the guise of accountability, who confronted a couple with a problem which wasn't really a problem. His explanation for supporting the gossip—the woman who heard from the wife of the couple, and who in turn told the pastor's wife out of "concern," who in turn told her husband, the pastor—was that the "gossiper" was in the right in doing what she did because she went to the one who "was responsible," namely him.

Again, Ken Blue points out,

> For leaders, gossip can also function as a means of control. Because these people are in the know, because they have their thumb on the pulse of the church, they can act as the authoritative clearinghouse for information....Pastoral gossip is one means of controlling the flow of information and maintaining power. Another effective means of information control is what one group refers to as "uplining." Uplining means that members of the group must bring all questions and concerns to the leader directly over them. They are never to discuss any problem with anyone other than this person. This leader is then to keep this concern to himself or pass it up to the leader above him. Such a closed system

enables the leaders to control the flow of information and to silence any person or issue they choose to....Healthy groups thrive on the free flow of information. Members have ready access to each other's opinions and concerns. Sick groups generally suffer from confused, defective or controlled communication. [5]

Question: can the concept of "responsibility" be abused? The answer is yes. Any over-aggrandizement of "responsibility" leads to a controlling and authoritarian condition. This was the case of this pastor. He saw himself as the one responsible to "fix" the problems that existed within his church. And that is the distortion; when an overly high and mighty sense of responsibility becomes Pharisaical. This is where we get the priesthood of the pastorate rather than the priesthood of all believers. They are the priests (the pastors), they hold the responsibility, and we are to submit...so the feeling goes.

> Any over-aggrandizement of "responsibility" leads to a controlling and authoritarian condition.

The fact of the matter is that we are all responsible one to the other, again, not as accountability cops but in building up the body of Christ. In addition, Scripture tells us to "work out your salvation in fear and trembling" (Phil. 2:12). We are to work it out and live it out. Our pastors and leaders aren't responsible for that. But, "control very well could be the Pharisees main addiction" [6] says John Fischer. Ultimately, when the "I am responsible" wand is waved over a congregation the root of the problem is probably a control issue. This problem however is self-perpetuating because of the Scriptural knowledge that pastors wield. It is at best intimidating!

Scriptural Intimidation

Probably the most powerful element of Pharisaical Leaders is their control over the people they serve with a command of Scripture that overwhelms their followers. Who can contend with someone who spent four years in Bible college, or worse yet, someone who spent an additional three years in seminary, not only learning theology, but Greek and Hebrew as well. Who can contend with someone who spends the greater majority of their week in Scripture, whether it be in preparation for a sermon or a Bible study? That is why my definition of a modern day Pharisee is ends with the phrase *"even when I use Scripture."*

This is where the Pharisees shined.

There is nothing that can control Christians more than a command of Scripture wrapped around a particular point of view.

Who could contend with them? They were the Scriptural experts, and they kept it meticulously on top of that! Their command of Scripture was so overwhelming that no matter what they said, those around them were pretty sure they were right. The Pharisees, confident of their command of the Scriptures even tried to trap Jesus, just waiting until they could prove that he was operating contrary to what God had said. Here is a small sampling of their kind of spiritual one-upmanship:

- *"Some Pharisees came to him to test him. They asked, "Is it lawful for a man to divorce his wife for any and every reason?" (Matthew 19:3)*
- *"Some of the Sadducees, who say there is no resurrection, came to Jesus with a question." (Luke 20:27)*
- *"Then the Pharisees went out and laid plans to trap him in his words."(Matthew 22:15)*

I guess they figured that if they could intimidate everyone else, surely they could intimidate the son of a carpenter. He, they were sure, would be no match for them! But, as Arterburn and Felton have pointed out, "Some of the most clever deceivers in history have used Scripture to foster their toxic faith. Satan had no problems in quoting Scripture...He used Scriptures from the Old Testament as tools for evil. The good guys are not the only ones who use Scripture!" [7]

Today, pastors and preacher/teachers have the same opportunity the Pharisees had, but even more so. They have an enormously intimidating platform in which they expound upon Scripture every week before their listening congregations. They are able to develop their thought patterns and construct their message in a way that is both appealing and convincing. If it sounds right, if it sounds logical, and if they present their sermons with a great deal of passion and conviction, people receive their message lock, stock, and barrel! Ultimately, people conclude: "he studied it, he's the professional, so it must be right."

There is nothing that can control Christians more than a command of Scripture wrapped around a particular point of view. It can be a robe of protection and a tool of manipulation. "But for some people the Word can become a god unto itself. Memorization can become an addiction rather than an act of devotion. Individuals become obsessed with verses and, in the process, forget that the verses are about a God who communicated his love to his people... The churchaholic obsessed with Scripture stops communicating because he or she fills every conversation with verses and sermonettes." [8] Twisting, turning, and using Scripture to one's own benefit has become an art form. And one that we should all be careful of. All it does is create a kind of Pharisaical control through intimidation.

The Bereans, on the other hand, had a different approach. They apparently questioned and challenged what Paul had to say. And their questioning brought them to investigate what he said for themselves. Acts 17:11 points out, "Now the Bereans were of more noble character than the Thessalonians, for they received the message with great eagerness and examined the Scriptures every day to see if what Paul said was true."

Paul is acknowledging what they did and encouraging all of us to do the same. Question, challenge, and investigate what is being taught. Check it out for yourselves. Don't just take for granted that what is being preached is 100% correct. It could be that there are aspects that what is being taught and communicated is not completely consistent with Scripture. It could be that the message is mostly right, but partly wrong. We need to be able to discern the difference.

This is a very threatening thing for many pastors. On the one hand, they want their people to get into Scripture more. I don't know of any pastor that doesn't. However, the concept of challenging and questioning what they have to say and preach smacks of rebellion and contention. They want unity and harmony, and the ability to preach what they have to say with boldness and absolute conviction. So how do you resolve these two competing issues?

Here are some guidelines that will help (but not alleviate) the tension between these two concepts:

1. Be a Berean Christian. Check out what is being preached as it squares with God's Word. This is YOUR responsibility.
2. Be extremely aware of the warning signs of Pharisaical Leaders who manipulate with Scripture. What are these warning signs and how do you know for sure if they are manipulation or passion?
    a. "Trust me." I have literally heard a pastor say, "Trust me," when being questioned about a direction a church was going. What is implied by an answer like this is "don't question me; I know I'm right, and you should agree with me. Besides, I am in authority, and what we want here is unity and peace!"

David Johnson and Jeff VanVonderen comment: "Though some in authority would love to never be questioned or opposed, the fact of the matter is that such a system is a trap and a downfall for any leader. If noticing problems is labeled disloyalty, lack of submission, divisiveness, and a challenge to authority, there is only a facade of peace and unity."[9]

b. Dominating: when a Pastor feels that he is called by God to exert ultimate control within a congregation; and when he is the exclusive selector of the elder board and ruling body, watch out. He may be creating a system that perpetuates Pharisaical domination over people. Contrary to this, as Ken Blue points out, "The New Testament writers seem oddly relaxed regarding church government and leadership. Unlike us, they appear to have little interest in determining who is in charge and how decisions are made. ...One thing is clear, however, and that is that the church during the New Testament era rejected hierarchy as its basic governmental structure. In Matthew 20:25 Jesus told his followers, "The rulers of the Gentiles lord it over them." That is to say, the world structures its institutions hierarchically, with those who rule dominating those who are ruled. He went on to say, "Not so with you.""[10]

c. Intimidating pressure: When a Pastor forces his opinion through manipulative and threatening words about his point of view, even using Scripture in the process, beware. Peter, as we mentioned, was briefly sucked into the Judaizers twisted use of Scripture to attempt to go back to the

132

law. It could have been very intimidating to stand up to Peter, the one who walked with Jesus so closely those three years; yet Paul saw through the situation, and knew what the Gospel was really all about. So he confronted Peter. "...Paul declared by this action that the truth always outranks position title in the church. Truth and its authority are not rooted in a personality or office. It is derived from the Word of God and the gospel it proclaims."[11]

A healthy Christian community is a Berean Christian community, one in which God's Word always trumps position, but that means challenging, debating, "contending for the truth." Interestingly enough, it also allows for diversity, various points of view, and different truths held in tension, and always, always, holding the truth in love.

Locked in

Part of a system that enables Pharisaical leadership to prosper is found in the reality that people are pretty much locked into their present environment and church body. To say it more clearly, if you want to fellowship in the church you are a part of, you better support what's going on. If you don't, you will be ostracized, alienated, or asked to leave. This is true of churches large and small. In the larger churches it is can take the form of a "take it or leave it" approach.

> To challenge what is being taught threatens your very security in the fellowship you love.

They may be so big that the potential loss of one family or member will not mean anything to them, and may not even be noticed. If it is a smaller church, you could get threatened with an insinuation that you are being divisive or going against God's ministry; that is, if you don't conform

133

completely to what is being said or done. In both cases the loss is yours.

The control is in the system. But Pharisaical environments are like that. The leaders are supported and enabled by the system they have set up, and even supported unwittingly or naturally by the followers who are in the church. David Johnson and Jeff VanVonderen comment:

> In shame-based systems, members have to deny any thought, opinion or feeling that is different than those of people in authority. Anything that has the potential to shame those in authority ignored or denied...problems are denied, and therefore they remain." [12] He clarifies this further: "followers sometimes obey or follow orders to avoid being shamed, to gain someone's approval, or to keep their spiritual status or church position intact. This is not true obedience or submission; it is compliant self-seeking. [13]

Perhaps you have come to Christ at this church, you have close friendships there, your children enjoy a dynamic youth ministry that has meaning to them, you have had many meaningful experiences within this particular church fellowship, all of this leading to one very powerful reality in your life: you are locked in, you are stuck! To challenge what is being taught threatens your very security in the fellowship you love. If you speak up, you may have to walk away from your support system. If this sounds a lot like a cult, it is. It is probably not a cult, but any environment which promotes a "don't talk" atmosphere is cultish.

Within Pharisaical environments people live their lives out in "quiet desperation" (Thoreau). People don't speak up, they keep quiet. Why rustle the feathers, upset the apple cart or stir the pot? All that does is come back to haunt you. No, better to be a good little Christian and keep quiet! Again, David Johnson and Jeff VanVonderen suggest:

> The most powerful of all unspoken rules in the abusive system is what we have already termed the "can't talk" rule....If you speak about the problem out loud, you are the problem...In abusive spiritual systems, there exists a "pretend peace"--what Jeremiah decreed, saying, "the prophets say 'peace, peace' when there is none." If what unites us is our pretending to agree, even though we don't agree, then we have nothing more than pretend peace and unity, with undercurrents of tension and backbiting. [14]

I once knew of an associate pastor who saw himself as the senior pastor's "protector". He took upon himself the responsibility to shield the senior pastor of any negative criticism. He felt that the pastor gets enough pot shots and criticism; he was empathetic to the reality that many people, who go out to lunch after church, have "roast pastor" along with their meal. He felt strongly that the pastor needs to be built up and supported, not "dragged down by criticism". So he felt that if he could "take the bullet" he could divert the harm or damage that would do to the pastor's psyche.

> Pharisees are good at turning around and manipulating a discussion to go their way.

While on the one hand, it is admirable that this guy wanted to "protect" and build up his pastor, on the other hand he may have prevented the pastor from hearing some things he needed to hear. Perhaps this pastor needs to hear something that is against the grain; or a divergent opinion. Under a system like this, under the guise of protection, this pastor is being set up for a Pharisaical dose of self-righteousness. This pastor's screener was the self-appointed judge who would determine what gets to the pastor and what does not. And the predominate message to

135

those whom he chose to filter was "Don't talk". Don't say anything that will hurt the pastor's ego, or undermine his agenda. As Johnson and VanVonderen observe: "The "can't-talk" rule, however, blames the person who talks, and the ensuing punishments pressure questioners into silence." [15]

Pharisees protect other Pharisees. They are a tightly knit group who alone know the burden of their responsibility and sacrifice. That's part of being locked in; the Pharisees have a support system that is stronger than yours. They protect and look out for each other. As John Fischer points out:

> The Pharisees traveled in a group, but it was not a group that told the truth. These kinds of groups foster a kind of collective, categorical blindness. Pharisees ... gangs ... Nazis ... it's the same principle. They travel in packs with clear rules about what you talk about and what you don't. These groups replace truth with propaganda—-a way of seeing the world that bolsters the false assumptions already made. [16]

Opponents are viewed as "instruments of the devil" or some other evil thing. When you go against one Pharisee you go against the whole bunch! Who do you think will prevail? If it's a matter of two sides to a story, their side is the one that will be considered credible. Knowing this, why fight it? So people remain quiet and "don't talk". Why put yourself into a position where YOU might be considered "evil" for correcting them?

You get locked in when the tables turn on you. You are not the victim, but the perpetrator. Instead of having insight or discernment, you are considered divisive, rebellious, and non-submissive. Pharisees are good at turning around and manipulating a discussion to go their way. Bring up an objection and they will tell you tell you where you failed, and they will bring Scripture in to support their view. You start out by talking about one thing, and in the end the Pharisee is talking about something altogether different and probably something that is YOUR problem.

I know about a pastor who said that he threw away negative comments and criticisms. He didn't belabor them or focus on them. He felt they were disruptive to God's ministry. This guy was a powerful force within his church. He was well liked and delivered a pretty good sermon. Why mess with the dissenters? Pharisees are good at crowd control. They only speak to those who will either agree with them, and promote the "don't talk" rule when they disagree. They preach to the choir. If you're not singing the same song, get out!

Quite frankly, I think it is difficult to be a pastor, and not be pulled into pharisaical tendencies. It is the Pharisaical Lure times ten. How can a pastor keep from becoming a Pharisee? Here are some guidelines:

1. Remember you are the servant:

    a. Don't be too impressed with your position

        "they love the place of honor at banquets and the most important seats in the synagogues; they love to be greeted in the marketplaces and to have men call them 'Rabbi.' "But you are not to be called 'Rabbi,' for you have only one Master and you are all brothers. (Matt. 23:6-8)

    b. Don't be confident in your own righteousness Jesus told the parable of the Pharisee and tax collector for this very reason: "To some who were confident of their own righteousness and looked down on everybody else, Jesus told this parable..." (Luke 18:9)

2. Be careful of the temptation to use manipulation and the power of intimidation:

a. Don't "lord it over" others, serve under them. "Jesus called them together and said, 'You know that the rulers of the Gentiles lord it over them, and their high officials exercise authority over them. Not so with you. Instead, whoever wants to become great among you must be your servant...'" (Matt. 20:25, 26)

b. Watch your word usage and getting your way by the way you handle Scripture. "The teachers of the law and the Pharisees sit in Moses' seat. So you must obey them and do everything they tell you. But do not d what they do, they do not practice what they preach. They tie up heavy loads and put them on men's shoulders..." (Matt. 23:2-4). Intimidation by using Scripture is a very heavy load for most that sit in the pew. They have to live with it...so they feel...guilty, pressured, and comply.

3. Create an environment of diversity and discussion; dialogue and debate; agreement and disagreement. Create a Berean environment (Acts 17:11), and an Athenian atmosphere, "So he reasoned in the synagogue with the Jews and the God-fearing Greeks..." (Acts 17:17) Be willing to hold some truths in tension, and the truth in love. If someone disagrees with you, consider their side, their view...really.

4. Don't allow yourself to be self-deceived:

a. "To some who were *confident* of their own righteousness" (as above, Luke 18:9) was an obvious statement of self-deception. Remember one of my definitions of the Pharisees at the beginning of this book: "They were self-deceived, spiritual technicians who looked for practical approaches on how to live the godly life."

b. The deception is that even in the pursuit of the godly life (after conversion) that we can somehow become righteous. Great "obedience" and knowledge never equate to righteousness. Never.

The best antidote for heavy loads is to lighten the load. That's why Jesus said, "My yoke is easy and my burden is light" (Matt. 11:30). The greatest thing any Christian leader can do is to lead his or her people to a fully engaged life of grace-full living. That's what a servant of the Lord does, because that's what Jesus did.

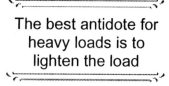

The best antidote for heavy loads is to lighten the load

Chapter 10

Grace-Full Living

"Shouldn't you have had mercy on your fellow servant just as I had on you?" Matthew 18:33

The question that everyone has been asking by now is: Where does this leave us? "If everyone tends toward self-righteousness, and ends up being a Pharisee, then this is a "no win" situation. What are we supposed to do now?"

This is of course a legitimate question, and hopefully these are the questions that have been rumbling within your heart and mind. You may be thinking that I have backed you into a corner, spiritually speaking, that no matter what you do, it is a helpless situation. You may have the feeling that you can't move, restricted by the mandate not to be restricting. You can no longer say anything to anybody for fear of being a Pharisee.

Those who are perpetual line drawers are very uncomfortable with this stuff. But no matter how you come to this, the prompting is the same…we beg for an answer, a definitive guideline on what we are to do. And so here it is:

Live out your life grace-fully!
That is your guideline and boundary!

It is the reality that you are to "work out your own salvation with fear and trembling" (Phil. 2:12). The concept here is to work out YOUR salvation…not someone else's. The unity that Paul talks about in Philippians 2:1-4, is not uniformity; nor is it to "have the same mind" of total agreement. The agreement here is precisely that YOU should work out your salvation and that others within the body work on theirs and you are each there to help and give support to each other. Support what *they* need, not what you impose upon them. It is about considering what others need from you, not a need which you demand them to have.

Grace-full living is the perfect antidote for our Pharisaical tendencies. It is hard to be a Pharisee when we live with a grace-full attitude—a real one that is. Here is what is involved in grace-full living:

1. The sense that we are all in the same boat.
2. A complete sense of thankfulness for what God has done in Christ.
3. A programmed resistance to legalism, self-righteousness, and judgementalism. A program to ward off these tendencies; a *Pharisee Prevention Program!*
4. An acceptance of messiness and a release of your right to judge; Grace received—Grace given.
5. Living each day for Him, fully, boldly, and freely.

We are all in the same boat

Here is the key to grace-full living, and the key to the concept of unity within the body of Christ. Pharisees think they are in one boat and everyone else is in another. They sail on the

Grace-full living involves knowing what boat you're in… It means trading in your righteousness card for a card which fully acknowledges who you are—a *Pharisee In Me* card spiritual ship of self-righteousness, while others are contaminated with the worlds concerns, on a ship filled with spiritual losers and misfits. The Pharisees, however, are in an exclusive fraternity, soaking in the rays of God's favor, simply because they are so good, so holy, and so righteous. But there is no grace to be found in their great virtue!

Grace-full living involves knowing what boat you're in. It means knowing who you are, and that everyone is the same. It means trading in your righteousness card for a card which fully acknowledges who you are—a *Pharisee In Me* card. With this card you board the same boat, the boat that sails upon the sea of grace. There is something freeing about acknowledging that you are a Pharisee. Simply acknowledging it keeps you from being the very Pharisee you admitted to being. When you look around, you will find that there are no favorites. In fact, you can only come on board if you've admitted to being a Pharisee...a sinner who cannot live a life free from sin, who cannot be righteous or holy in him or her self, a person who has done nothing to achieve a better position than the other.

For all the line-drawers of the world, you have to see that Jesus really only drew one line. It was not a line we Pharisees would normally expect. The line he drew was one where on the one side were those who felt they could cast the first stone; on the other side was everyone else...the sinners who deserved to have stones cast at them. The Pharisees realized that day that they could not cast the first stone. They could not say that they were without sin...any sin; not just a similar sin to the woman caught in adultery, but *any* sin. And when, as we have discussed before, he dismantled the act of sin to equal a sinful thought, well that pretty much puts everyone in the same boat. But in order to sail on that boat, you have to admit...not that you sin, that's too easy, but to admit that your sin is just as bad as everyone else's sin, which then, puts you on the same boat.

Now you can look around, and see pastors, missionaries, elders and deacons, and everyone else who comes to Christ seeking to be free from their yoke of slavery. Everyone is in the same boat, even those previously thought of as spiritual giants. This is the true kind of unity present in a grace-full life, and this is what it means to be of "one mind."

A complete sense of thankfulness

Grace-full living is thankful living. In the first place, you are thankful that you are even on this boat. You know that you don't deserve it, knowing who you are; you wonder why YOU of all people were chosen to be here. You look at what Christ has done for you and everyone else on this boat and are amazed at HIS grace.

It's hard to be a Pharisee when you're in the midst of thankfulness. Self-righteousness can't be found in the presence of thankfulness. It's not like the Pharisee who said, "I thank you Lord that I am not like that sinner (tax-collector)"; it's just the opposite. It's more like, "I am thankful, because I'm just like that tax-collector; but I have acted like the Pharisee; and now I see the self-righteousness that is in me. But, in spite of that, you have saved me too! I'm thankful, because I'm not as worthy as the tax-collector. I don't always realize my sin and often promote my own sense of holiness. I am in the same boat as the tax-collector; and like him I say, 'Lord, be merciful to me, a sinner'. And like him, you have shown me your mercy and grace. Thank you, thank you, thank you!"

John Fischer says:

> The giving of thanks is the only logical response one can have to a forgiveness and a holiness that are totally undeserved.

By nature of the fact that grace is a gift, there is nothing one can do but receive it and be thankful for it. Thankfulness is so tied to grace that the absence of gratitude in a Christian's life is an indication that legalism still rules the day...We have done nothing to deserve, create, or maintain the righteousness we have been given, and therefore we can do nothing but be grateful for it.[1]

Developing a program that resists self-righteousness. A Pharisee Prevention Program.

While I don't like the rigidity of programs, I do like the organization that programs bring to my life. That's why I think people all over the world flock to self-help programs, "How to" programs, "12 step" programs, and so on. I abhor any concept that provides five easy steps to victory or seven steps to success because life is never that simple, and success is not just a matter of following a few steps someone has laid down. I am committed to the concept of God's sovereignty over all of life…and over my life. Because I acknowledge his sovereignty, I must live my life with the belief and acceptance that He will ultimately direct my course.

However, having said that, I like a program that guides me, and reinforces my directions, allegiances, and changes my behavior. Steven Covey's *Seven Habits of Highly Effective People* is good because when I "work the program" my life is lived on purpose; and Rick Warren's book, *Purpose Driven Life* succeeds because he enables me to construct my purpose around God's purpose, all the while knowing that God has the final word in what happens to me. For this reason, it is my belief that we need to create a program that will thwart our tendencies toward self-righteousness, legalism, and judgementalism.

I do not for one minute believe that this book will be enough to end or even begin to stalemate the enormous g-forces that have built up in our lives, which continuously push us towards these tendencies. We need something more powerful than a book. That's why we have created a "program" which will bring this topic to the forefront of a church or fellowship. A study program actually was developed before the creation of this book by the same name: *Thank God I'm Not a Pharisee...or am I?*

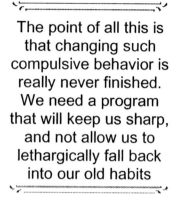

The point of all this is that changing such compulsive behavior is really never finished. We need a program that will keep us sharp, and not allow us to lethargically fall back into our old habits

The title is obviously a facetious jab emphasizing the reality of it all. What is obvious is that no one wants to become a Pharisee; but what is the reality is that we do so without realizing it. It is really quite an easy thing to become a Pharisee. The title is a little "off center" to hopefully catch your attention; if you are reading this book, that has been accomplished. But the program we have developed suggests that a church study group or home group address this subject matter for as much as six to eight weeks! Now, if anything can help us begin to resist our Pharisaical tendencies it is dealing with the subject for a period of time that is sufficient for the full weight of it to begin to sink in. The program provides a DVD which will guide a class or home group through each part of the "process" and a *Study Guide* will bring the participants into a challenging and confrontational, yet honest discussion and dialogue.

But even that's not enough. Something has got to grab our attention and awareness on a daily basis. It is for that reason we have developed the *Pharisee Prevention Handbook* and the *Pharisee In Me* card, reinforcement tools that will both remind us daily of our tendencies toward Pharisaicalism and to catch us in the act of being Pharisaical.[‡]

[‡] you can order these tools from *Reality Check Recourses* at www.realitycheckresources.com

The point of all this is that changing such compulsive behavior is really never finished. We need a program that will keep us sharp, and not allow us to lethargically fall back into our old habits. This helps in the process of becoming mature and loving Christians—never arriving, always developing, always on the offensive so that we might "work out our own salvation in fear and trembling."

That's why it is near impossible to "do" the fruit of the spirit. Once I think I've got one thing "worked out" I realize I'm weak in another. So I start working on "that thing" and I begin to become weak in the very thing I previously worked on. It never ends. It is not about "doing something" or "doing good works" in the way that the work is like a goal that is accomplished or completed. It is not something you check off your life. It is more like the process of becoming. Any way you look at the need for *Pharisee Prevention* has never been greater and it is our hope that with the aid of our support tools never been more possible.

Grace received—Grace given...an acceptance of messiness

There is nothing as attractive as grace and nothing as repulsive as judgementalism. Most of us are attracted to Christ by His irresistible grace, a grace that is incomprehensible,

> There is nothing as attractive as grace and nothing as repulsive as judgementalism.

unconditional, and amazing! We live our lives in response to His amazing grace and tell others of how thankful we are that He doesn't condemn us because of our sin.

Yet, why is it that we don't offer the same generosity to others? In the *Pharisee Prevention Handbook* I ask this question: "Are you granting to the offender as much grace as has been given to you?" Jesus confronted the judgers, line-drawers, and even his disciples with this question in the parable of the Unmerciful Servant in Matthew 18:21-35. He says, "shouldn't you have [had] mercy on your fellow servant

146

as I have on you?" We don't like that question, but we know it's true, so we say, "Yes, but…" He or she needs to "understand"…He or she needs to know the line if they are going to tow the line"…He or she doesn't "do_____enough".

"Yes, but…" is just another aspect of the *"not enough"* syndrome. And it is our excuse for not offering as much mercy as has been offered to us. As long as we can put a "yes, but" to qualify our acceptance of someone we only offer a conditional, safe, rigid and minimal kind of mercy. God's grace covers all; but our grace has some standards which must be met first. We're thankful for the canceling of our debt, but our fellow servants, they must pay theirs!

Let's face it: we have a problem canceling debts, if the debt—what is still owed—isn't paid. It's hard "to look the other way." Every bone in our body cries out, "but she needs to pay for what she's done". Like spiritual accountants we want to know that the books are balanced. And we want to make sure that no one "cooks the books." Instead of accepting that we are all "in the red," and that we are all spiritually bankrupt, we want to reveal the ledger in each others lives.

Now I bet the minute some who read this statement wanted to qualify it with a conditional kind of mercy. You may be thinking, "Yes, but a person can't keep on filing bankruptcy or they are taking advantage of the system." That's cheap grace!

Mike Yaconelli understood that the grace we receive in Christ is not cheap, it's priceless. It can never be paid back. Even our feeble attempts at righteousness pale in comparison. We will never balance the books, never "even the scales," and never come even remotely close to getting out of the red; as far as our righteousness is concerned. His book on *Messy Spirituality* makes the case for the fact that we cannot even up the score. In fact, all of our righteousness is but filthy rags…dirty, tattered, torn, and incomplete. We will never even the score! It is only when we realize this that we will *give out* grace because of the grace that has been given to us; we will distribute grace generously, abundantly, profusely, and at every opportunity. We will give out more grace than righteousness, more grace than law, more grace than obedience, more grace than holiness, more grace than we think should ever be given.

When we begin to think about law, and give out grace, we sacrifice our lines; when we begin to think about righteousness and give out grace, we sacrifice our standards; when we begin to think about obedience and give out grace, we sacrifice our need to see a neat and tidy Christian who conforms to our image, our demands, our lines, and our judgments. And when we feel the sacrifice of our grace we offer to someone who we think "should" be different, better, more holy, more spiritual, we hand back the measuring stick, the accounting form, that balancing scale to Jesus Christ who of course is the only one who can use them properly. As John Fischer said, "There is really only one cure to this addiction [to self-righteousness]: (1) to realize who God is and how beyond our control are his ways, (2) to see that the end of what we work for apart from him is all without worth, and (3) to accept that there is nothing for us to measure except the immeasurable grace of God—no one to compare ourselves to but Christ. The first is what leads us to worship, the second is what leads us to depend on him for everything, and the third is what unites us with everyone else." [2]

> Grace-full living is living each day, boldly and freely for Him.

Of all the things Jesus Christ sacrificed it was not the terror and torture of his flesh being beaten; it was not the giving up of his solely Godly nature to take on human flesh; it was not the endurance of temptations that confront humans; rather it was the sacrifice of grace. He gave something that WAS NOT AND WILL NOT EVER BE DESERVED OR EARNED. That's a sacrifice of ultimate and extreme proportion!

Now..."shouldn't you have mercy on your fellow servant just as I had on you?" Go ahead, try, and just try to do the same!

Living each day for Him

Grace-full living is living each day, boldly and freely for Him. When we sacrifice our need to draw lines, expect obedience, and be legalistic and judgmental, all we are left with is ourselves and the life we have to live. That then frees us up to live our lives in a much fuller way. Unencumbered by the need to apply any righteousness of my own to others, I can now concentrate on what God has saved me *for*, and what God has called me *to*.

The real question in life is what has God saved me *for*? The Westminster Confession asked it this way: "What is the chief end of man?" Answer: "To love God and enjoy Him forever." Out of the freedom that Christ has given me—free from condemnation, free from the bondage of self-righteousness, free from legalism, free from judging and being judged; I can more freely live my life for Him.

Grace-full living is a life lived under the umbrella of His grace and with nothing other than a desire to live for Him. The words of Scripture confirm this: "Whatever you do, work at it with all your heart, as working for the Lord, not for men." (Col. 3:23). Why can we do this? Because He "qualified you" (Col. 1:12)! He qualified you, not someone else. We work for Him, not others. The motivation and passion of our life is to please Him, to work for Him, to glorify Him in ALL we do. As Georg Huntemann suggests, "Rather, being in the midst of the world and at the same time living as Jesus' disciple means that the Christian has the responsibility to live daily under the forgiveness of the cross. Costly grace is lived-out grace..." [3]

Out of this framework we live in a strange juxtaposition of life. There is a sense that we sin boldly. Not sin deliberately, but boldly. It is not "sin that grace

> Rather, mixed in with my sinfulness and sinful tendencies; there is still this overwhelming desire and motivation to please God

may abound;" rather, because grace abounds, I can live freely and fully. Hebrews 4:16 relates to us that we can "with confidence" or "boldly" come before the throne of grace.

As I've said earlier, if I spent my whole life trying to rid myself of sin, I wouldn't be able to do anything. However, I have the confidence that the Holy Spirit is doing His work in me...even when I'm unaware. I know that I am a sinner—both positionally and in my daily actions; and I know that I will sin at the drop of a hat. Today, I may lust, covet, be angry, neglect someone, or commit other relapses into my tendency toward sinfulness. If I lived with a sense of uptightness or paranoia about this, I would end up in a paralyzing state of non-effectiveness. I would be worthless. Bob George, in his book, *Classic Christianity*, adds:

> Under law you never experience peace or rest in the Christian life. Why? Because your work is never done. A spiritual restlessness results, where you are always looking for the something more that will transform your Christian life into reality. It's always around the corner: at the next seminar, in the next book, in finding that spiritual experience—never resting in Christ Himself who lives in you, who has already done it who has given you everything you need.[4]

Rather, mixed in with my sinfulness and sinful tendencies; there is still this overwhelming desire and motivation to please God; and that motivation encompasses my whole entire life. To live fully for Him is to live for Him within the context of my everyday activities...out in the real world. It is not, as some have suggested; to live life with some other kind of spiritual agenda that I add to my life in order to make it spiritually legitimate. I do not need to make work my ministry, or to think "evangelism" at every encounter.

Pharisees want to spiritualize everything, making a normal life "acceptable" only if it is somehow has a "higher" purpose than what it really is. Pharisees divide life into compartments: the sacred and the secular, the spiritual and the unspiritual, doing eternal things and doing carnal things, the holy and the unholy, the things that count and the things that are necessary. Work becomes necessary; evangelism is the thing that counts; prayer is a holy activity while making a sales call is unholy and carnal; Bible study of course is spiritual but studying science or business is secular; and so on.

Those that occupy the "spiritual professions", like pastors, evangelists, and missionaries, are the spiritual ones, while those who occupy all the other professions, well, they need to be more spiritual! Pharisaical living divides life between the spiritual 'haves' and the lowly 'have-nots'.

Grace-full living on the other hand views all of life to be lived under the freeing and empowering umbrella of God's grace. Understanding that, I can pursue my work life, my entertainment, my study, my recreation, my sports, my church life, my Bible study, my witnessing, my prayer life, my whatever…all freely, and fully for Him.

> Grace-full living on the other hand views all of life to be lived under the freeing and empowering umbrella of God's grace

Bach signed his work "Soli Deo Groria," "Glory to the Lamb." In his treatise, A Prelude concerning the Babylonian Captivity of the Church, Luther said "The works of monks and priests, however holy and arduous they be, do not differ one whit in the sight of God from the works of the rustic laborer in the field or the woman going about her household tasks, but that all words are measured before God by faith alone." (As quoted by Os Guinness in his book, The Call) And Abraham Kuyper said, "There is not a single square inch in the entire universe of which Christ, the sovereign Lord of all, does not say, 'This is mine!'"

The point is that our whole life is spiritual, sacred, and devoted to God. Every activity counts and matters to God. It is all dedicated to Him and for His eternal purpose. And it is all holy, meaningful, and can be lived to His Glory. The guy who collects my garbage, if he is a Christian, is as special and spiritual as the elder at my church who attends every activity the church has to offer. The teacher who teaches my children, if he or she is a Christian is as spiritual as my Pastor. The banker, who handles my money, if he or she is a Christian, is as spiritual as the missionary who has dedicated his life to spreading the gospel in a foreign country. You count as much to God as Billy Graham, or Bill Hybels, or Rick Warren, or as your local pastor, or as any of the other spiritual icons you can point to. Grace-full living knows this, believes this, and lives this.

For those icons of spirituality that roam the halls of spiritual acceptability, "beware the yeast of the Pharisees;" the yeast may be in you. To live grace-fully is to accept, without any other pretense, the fact that the person you are trying so hard to be is no better than any other Christian. And to all of the "other" persons out there who compare themselves to these spiritual icons: understand that you can live unencumbered by those comparisons simply by knowing that in God's eyes you are no less than they.

The significance in knowing this is that YOU CAN LIVE FREELY, and be YOU unashamedly! Free to be the banker because you were called to BE a banker, not a missionary. Free to be a garbage collector because garbage needs to be collected and is a great service to the community. Free to be a stay at home mother and housewife, because he called you to BE a Christian mother and housewife, not an evangelist. Free to be a business person, not a preacher, because He called YOU to BE a business person. No other agenda is needed. You do not need to legitimize your banking by spending every waking hour away from the bank at church. You do not need to think as a garbage collector that somehow if you could also be an elder then there would be some spiritual worth to your life. A mother and housewife does not need to wish she was a missionary, so she could be pleasing to God. And a business person does not need to evangelize at work to legitimize his place in the world.

The Heidelberg Catechism divided realities of our life into three dimensions: Sin, Salvation, and Service. We are conceived and born into sin and have inherited the sinful nature and disposition of Adam. We are incapable of any righteousness of our own. Those who have accepted by faith the grace offered to become righteous only through the sacrifice and resurrection of Jesus Christ live their life with a sense of what He has done and what He is doing. The Holy Spirit now, through His regeneration process; motivates, stimulates, invigorates, and unchains us to live life for His service. Our whole, entire life is now a life of service *to* Him and *for* Him. All that we do is FOR God and we can do it GRACE-FULLY!

It is my sincere hope and prayer, that through this book, and perhaps with the aid of the video series, you have been able to forgo any sense of denial, accept the tendency to be legalistic, self-righteous, and judgmental and realize how easy it is to be a Pharisee. Armed with a programmed resistance to the Pharisaical lifestyle, and robed with the cloak of Christ's grace; I am confident that you can and will offer to others the grace that has been given to you!

God Bless You.

John Elzinga, 2005

Bibliography and Suggested Reading

The books below are also noted in the endnotes. I recommend them all. I wanted you to know why, and so I use this small section to provide you some insight into why I think these books are useful. Enjoy and discover:

William Barclay, *The Gospel of Matthew, Volume 1 and 2,* Philadelphia, Westminster Press, Revised Edition, 1975

I drew heavily on the information and insight provided by Barclay's commentaries. I would suggest that any serious study of Pharisees the student should at least get a copy of The Gospel of Matthew volumes 1 and 2.

Dietrich Bonhoeffer, *The Cost of Discipleship* New York:The Macmillan Company, 1949

If you have read this classic also read, *The Other Bonhoeffer* by Georg Huntemann—see below. He provides insights that may surprise you.

Jacques Ellul, *Propaganda.The Formation of Men's Attitudes* New York: Vintage Books, a division of Random House, 1965

Although Ellul is a French Christian, this is not a "Christian" book. It is a sociological book which examines how we develop paradigms from a cultural point of view. The pertenence here is that church fellowships are tightly formed communities which tend to develop certain attitudes, feelings, and behaviors over against others (on the outside). It is this 'over-againstness' which is phaisaical.

John Fischer, *12 Steps for the Recovering Pharisee (like me), Finding Grace to Live Unmasked*, Minneapolis, Minnesota, Bethany Press International, 2000

John Fischer's book is a must get book. You can get it on Amazon.com as well as other sources. His metaphoric way of comparing our addiction to a Pharisaical life style to a twelve step program gets right to the point of what I call the Pharisaical Lure.

Bob George, *Classic Christianity* Eugene, Oregon: Harvest House, 1989
A book which emphasizes grace over works—what a relief!

Georg Huntemann, *The Other Bonhoeffer,* Grand Rapids, Michigan: Baker Books, 1993

You will be surprised by some of the things Huntemann reveals about Bonhoeffer. His insight is worth investigating.

Lewis B. Smedes, *A Pretty Good Person*, HarperSanFrancisco, New York, 1990
Lewis B. Smedes, *How Can It Be All Right When Everything Is All Wrong*, Colorado Springs, WaterBrook Press, Colorado, 1982, 1999.

Both of Lewis Smedes' books relate an understanding of the common Christian who has common problems, common questions, and common frustrations. They nurture the reader with an under-girding of God's grace.

Dallas Willard, Book, *The Divine Conspiracy* New York, New York: HarperSanFrancisco, 1998

Dallas Willard has a wonderful way of turning everything around so that we can look at it from another angle. This book will change the way you think about so many things.

Michael Yaconelli, *Messy Spirituality, God's Annoying Love for Imperfect People*, Grand Rapids, Michigan, Zondervan, 2002

Mike Yaconelli's book is particularly appropriate because it takes a load of guilt off those of us who are normal, run of the mill, sinful Christians who daily need a dose of God's grace to keep us going.

For those of you who are leaders, elders, deacons, and pastors in your local congregation I would suggest getting the following books. You see, it is easier to become a Pharisee in a leadership position.

The Arbinger Institute, *Leadership and Self-Deception,* San Francisco: Berrett-Loehler Publishers, Inc., 2000

While this is not a "Christian" book, it uncovers how leaders overlook their own involvement in organizational problems. I've recommended it to many leaders.

Stephen Arterburn & Jack Felton, *Toxic Faith*, Colorado Springs, Colorado: WaterBrook Press, 1991, 2001

Arterburn and Felton tell it like it is. Toxic is the right word to describe self-righteousness and its sickening affect upon the local Church fellowship. To those leaders who can handle it, I recommend you read this book.

Ken Blue, *Healing Spiritual Abuse, How to Break Free from Bad Church Experiences*, Downers Grove, Illinois, Intervarsity Press, 1993

David Johnson and Jeff VanVonderen, *The Subtle Power of Spiritual Abuse, Recognizing and Escaping Spiritual Manipulations and False Spiritual Authority Within the Church*, Minneapolis, Minnesota, Bethany House Publishers, 1991

If you are in leadership in any capacity within the local church I highly recommend you read both books: *Healing Spiritual Abuse* by Ken Blue and *The Subtle Power of Spiritual Abuse* by Johnson and VanVonderen. Don't read one or the other, read them both. They rightfully address the issue that Pharisaical self-righteousness and judgementalism is particularly susceptible to those who are leaders.

NOTES

Chapter One

1. Lewis B. Smedes, *A Pretty Good Person* (New York, New York: HarperSanFrancisco, 1990), 74
2. Lewis B. Smedes, *A Pretty Good Person* (New York, New York: HarperSanFrancisco, 1990), 138

Chapter Two

1. I am not intending to go into a theological debate about tongues, prophesy, and healing. What I am intending to do is comment on spiritual arrogance that so easily surrounds these subjects.

Chapter Three

1. Reprinted from *How Can It Be All Right When Everything Is All Wrong?* p. 167,168, Copyright © 1999 by Lewis B. Smedes. Used by permission of WaterBrook Press, Colorado Springs, CO. All rights reserved.
2. John Fischer, *12 Steps for the Recovering Pharisee (Like me)* (Minneapolis, Minnesota: Bethany House, a division of Baker Publishing Group, 2000), 11

Chapter Four

1. Reprinted from *Toxic Faith* p.103,104 Copyright © 1991, 2001 by Stephen Arterburn & Jack Felton. Used by permission of WaterBrook Press Colorado Springs, CO. All rights reserved.
2. The characteristic of yeast is that it invades the dough. It dominates it; it takes over; and it becomes the controlling factor for the dough "rising". Ultimately, you can't separate the yeast from the dough because it is the predominate ingredient which changes the structure (and the life) of the dough. So it is with us.
3. John Fischer, *12 Steps for the Recovering Pharisee (Like me)* (Minneapolis, Minnesota: Bethany House, a division of Baker Publishing Group, 2000), 11
4. The Arbinger Institute, *Leadership and Self-Deception* (San Francisco: Berrett-Koehler Publishers, Inc., 2000), 16
5. The Arbinger Institute, *Leadership and Self-Deception* (San Francisco: Berrett-Koehler Publishers, Inc., 2000), 40

Chapter Five

1. Reprinted from *How Can It Be All Right When Everything Is All Wrong?* p.38, Copyright © 1999 by Lewis B. Smedes. Used by permission of WaterBrook Press, Colorado Springs, CO. All rights reserved.
2. John Fischer, *12 Steps for the Recovering Pharisee (like me)* (Minneapolis, Minnesota: Bethany House, a division of Baker Publishing Group, 2000), 92
3. Taken from: *Classic Christianity* by Bob George Copyright © 2000 by Harvest House Publishers, Eugene, OR, Used by Permission, www.harvesthousepublishers.com, 139
4. Dallas Willard, *The Divine Conspiracy* (New York, New York: HarperSanFrancisco, 1998), 106
5. John Fischer, *12 Steps for the Recovering Pharisee (like me)* (Minneapolis, Minnesota: Bethany House, a division of Baker Publishing Group, 2000), 35

Chapter Six

1. Michael Yaconelli, *Messy Spirituality; God's Annoying Love for Imperfect People* (Grand Rapids, Michigan: Zondervan, 2002), Back Cover of book
2. Taken from: *Classic Christianity* by Bob George Copyright © 2000 by Harvest House Publishers, Eugene, OR, Used by Permission, www.harvesthousepublishers.com, 148
3. John Fischer, *12 Steps for the Recovering Pharisee (like me)* (Minneapolis, Minnesota: Bethany House, a division of Baker Publishing Group, 2000), 16
4. Michael Yaconelli, *Messy Spirituality; God's Annoying Love for Imperfect People* (Grand Rapids, Michigan: Zondervan, 2002), 12,13
5. Dallas Willard, *The Divine Conspiracy* (New York, New York: HarperSanFrancisco, 1998), 41
6. John Fischer, *12 Steps for the Recovering Pharisee (like me)* (Minneapolis, Minnesota: Bethany House, a division of Baker Publishing Group, 2000), 45
7. Adapted from a story called "You Need 100 Points," posted on www.inhis.com

Chapter Seven

1. Jacques Ellul, *Propaganda.The Formation of Men's Attitudes* (New York: Vintage Books, Alfred A. Knopf, Inc.,a division of Random House, 1965), 63,64

2. Jacques Ellul, *Propaganda.The Formation of Men's Attitudes* (New York: Vintage Books, Alfred A. Knopf, Inc., a division of Random House, 1965), 100

3. Jacques Ellul, *Propaganda.The Formation of Men's Attitudes* (New York: Vintage Books, Alfred A. Knopf, Inc., a division of Random House, 1965), 111

4. William Barclay, commentary, *The Daily Study Bible Series* (Philadelphia: The Westminster Press, 1975), 292

5. Dallas Willard, *The Divine Conspiracy* (New York, New York: HarperSanFrancisco, 1998), 133

6. David Johnson & Jeff VanVonderen, *The Subtle Power of Spiritual Abuse* (Minneapolis, Minnesota: Bethany House, a division of Baker Publishing Group, 1991), 23

Chapter Eight

1. William Barclay, commentary, *The Daily Study Bible Series* (Philadelphia: The Westminster Press, 1975), 189, translation of Rom. 14:13-16

2. John Fischer, *12 Steps for the Recovering Pharisee (like me)* (Minneapolis, Minnesota: Bethany House, a division of Baker Publishing Group, 2000), 46

3. Reprinted with the permission of Scribner, an imprint of Simon & Schuster Adult Publishing Group, from the COST OF DISCIPLESHIP by Dietrich Bonhoeffer. Copyright © 1959 by SCM Press Ltd., 47,48

4. Bonhoffer, D., *Letters and Papers from Prison*, New York: The Macmillan Company, 1972, 369 as quoted in Huntemann, G., *The Other Bonhoffer,* Grand Rapids, MI: Baker Book House, 1993, 77.

5. Bonhoffer, D., *The Cost of Discipleship*, New York: The Macmillan Company, 1963, 57,58 as quoted in Huntemann, G., *The Other Bonhoffer,* Grand Rapids, MI: Baker Book House, 1993, 187.

6. Bonhoffer, D., *Letters and Papers from Prison*, New York: The Macmillan Company, 1972, 346 as quoted in Huntemann, G., *The Other Bonhoffer,* Grand Rapids, MI: Baker Book House, 1993, 189.

7. Dallas Willard, *The Divine Conspiracy* (New York, New York: HarperSanFrancisco, 1998), 219, 221

8. Taken from "Healing Spiritual Abuse" by Ken Blue. Copyright (c) 1993 by Ken Blue. Used with permission of InterVarsity Press, P.O. Box 1400, Downers Grove, IL 60515. www.ivpress.com, 47

Chapter Nine

1. Taken from "Healing Spiritual Abuse" by Ken Blue. Copyright (c) 1993 by Ken Blue. Used with permission of InterVarsity Press, P.O. Box 1400, Downers Grove, IL 60515. www.ivpress.com, 28,29
2. Editor Michael Scott Horton, *Power Religion* (Chicago: Moody Press, 1992), 19 [please note, Ken Blue, in his book noted above also references this quote from Michael Horton on page 28 in *Healing Spiritual Abuse*]
3. David Johnson & Jeff VanVonderen, *The Subtle Power of Spiritual Abuse* (Minneapolis, Minnesota: Bethany House, a division of Baker Publishing Group, 1991), 112
4. Taken from "Healing Spiritual Abuse" by Ken Blue. Copyright (c) 1993 by Ken Blue. Used with permission of InterVarsity Press, P.O. Box 1400, Downers Grove, IL 60515. www.ivpress.com, 35
5. Taken from "Healing Spiritual Abuse" by Ken Blue. Copyright (c) 1993 by Ken Blue. Used with permission of InterVarsity Press, P.O. Box 1400, Downers Grove, IL 60515. www.ivpress.com, 73,74
6. John Fischer, *12 Steps for the Recovering Pharisee (like me)* (Minneapolis, Minnesota: Bethany House, a division of Baker Publishing Group, 2000), 47
7. Reprinted from *Toxic Faith* p.137 Copyright © 1991, 2001 by Stephen Arterburn & Jack Felton. Used by permission of WaterBrook Press Colorado Springs, CO. All rights reserved.
8. Reprinted from *Toxic Faith* p.99,100 Copyright © 1991, 2001 by Stephen Arterburn & Jack Felton. Used by permission of WaterBrook Press Colorado Springs, CO. All rights reserved.
9. David Johnson & Jeff VanVonderen, *The Subtle Power of Spiritual Abuse* (Minneapolis, Minnesota: Bethany House, a division of Baker Publishing Group, 1991), 69
10. Taken from "Healing Spiritual Abuse" by Ken Blue. Copyright (c) 1993 by Ken Blue. Used with permission of InterVarsity Press, P.O. Box 1400, Downers Grove, IL 60515. www.ivpress.com, 141
11. Taken from "Healing Spiritual Abuse" by Ken Blue. Copyright (c) 1993 by Ken Blue. Used with permission of InterVarsity Press, P.O. Box 1400, Downers Grove, IL 60515. www.ivpress.com, 30
12. David Johnson & Jeff VanVonderen, *The Subtle Power of Spiritual Abuse* (Minneapolis, Minnesota: Bethany House, a division of Baker Publishing Group, 1991), 58

13. David Johnson & Jeff VanVonderen, *The Subtle Power of Spiritual Abuse* (Minneapolis, Minnesota: Bethany House, a division of Baker Publishing Group, 1991), 66

14. David Johnson & Jeff VanVonderen, *The Subtle Power of Spiritual Abuse* (Minneapolis, Minnesota: Bethany House, a division of Baker Publishing Group, 1991), 68

15. David Johnson & Jeff VanVonderen, *The Subtle Power of Spiritual Abuse* (Minneapolis, Minnesota: Bethany House, a division of Baker Publishing Group, 1991), 68

16. John Fischer, *12 Steps for the Recovering Pharisee (like me)* (Minneapolis, Minnesota: Bethany House, a division of Baker Publishing Group, 2000), 31

Chapter Ten

1. John Fischer, *12 Steps for the Recovering Pharisee (like me)* (Minneapolis, Minnesota: Bethany House, a division of Baker Publishing Group, 2000), 143

2. John Fischer, *12 Steps for the Recovering Pharisee (like me)* (Minneapolis, Minnesota: Bethany House, a division of Baker Publishing Group, 2000), 47

3. Huntemann, G., *The Other Bonhoffer,* Grand Rapids, MI: Baker Book House, 1993, 187.

4. Taken from: *Classic Christianity* by Bob George Copyright ©2000 by Harvest House Publishers, Eugene, OR, Used by Permission, www.harvesthousepublishers.com, 146

If you would like to find out more about John Elzinga and Reality Check Resources please go to his web site at www.realitycheckresources.com. You may also contact him or his agent, Lorin Ganske, about the possibility of having John come to speak at your church or organization at 1-800-671-2011.

John Elzinga
1002 5th St SE
Orange City, IA. 51041
johnelzinga@frontier.com

Printed in the United States
44961LVS00007BB/172-510

9 781597 819084